It's Complicated

Crazy Drawings by
Kimberly Garvey

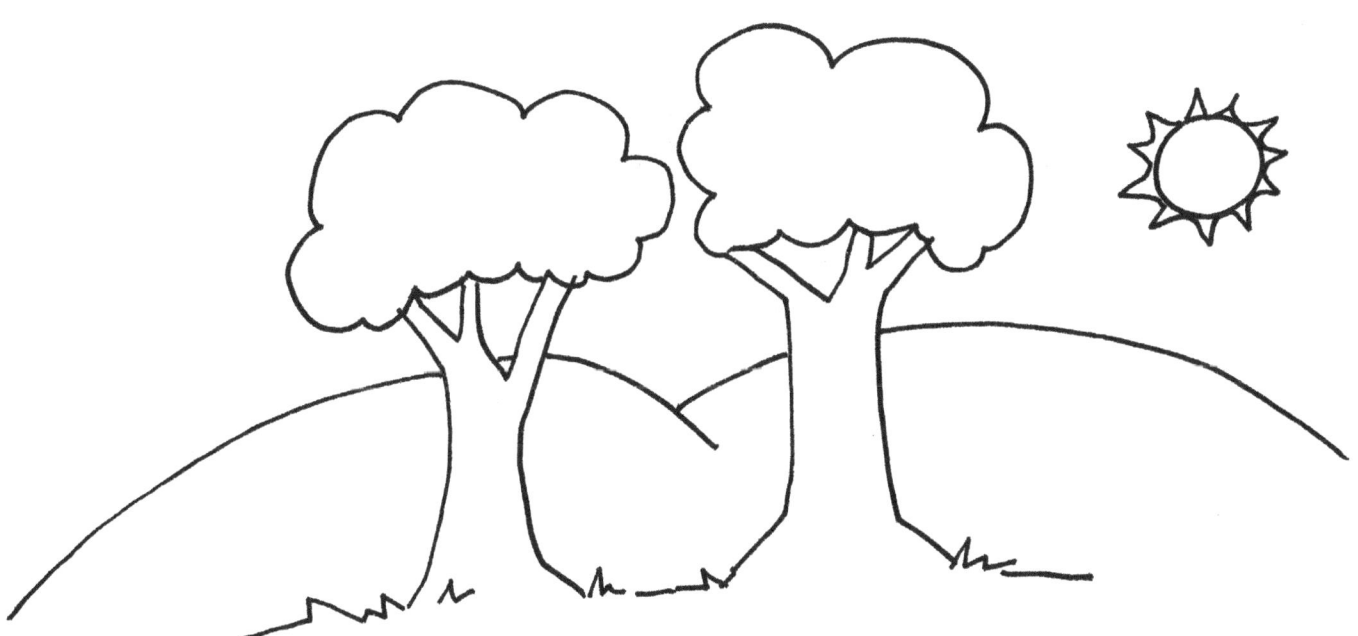

A COLORING BOOK FOR THE DARING COLORING ARTIST

Kimberlygarvey.com

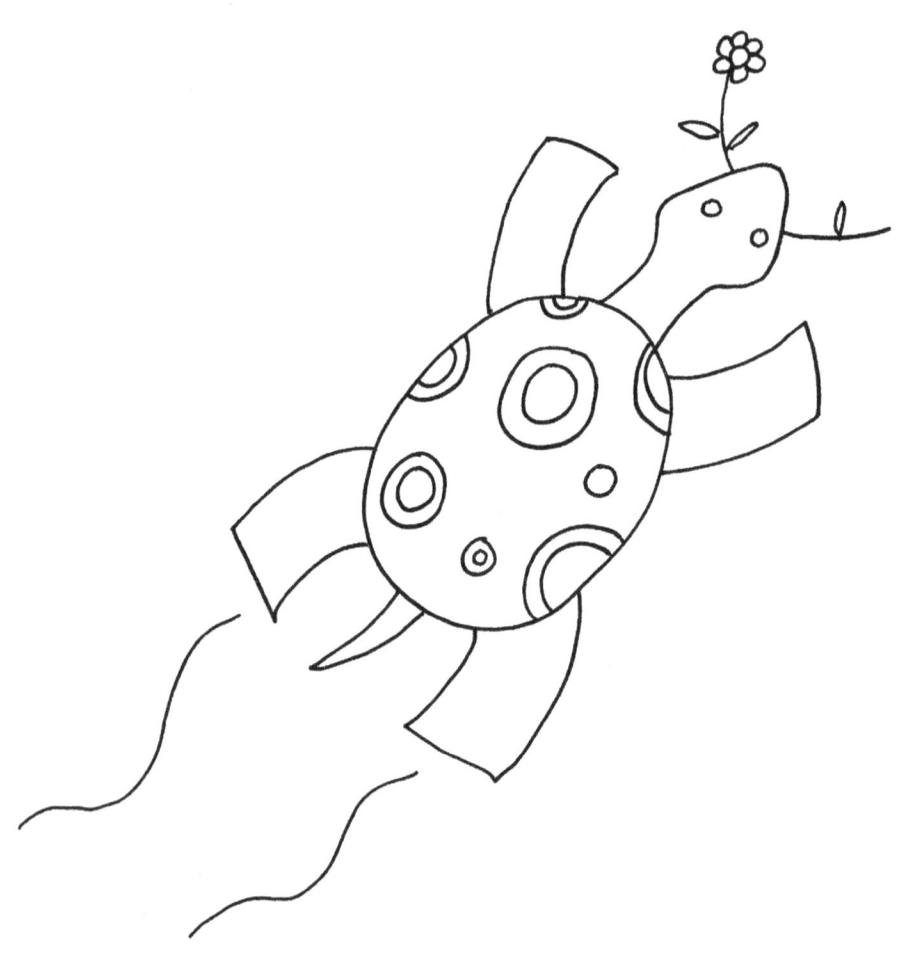

WARNING!!!!

Please put a protection sheet of paper between the pages when using markers to prevent bleed-through.

A protection sheet is included at the back of this book.

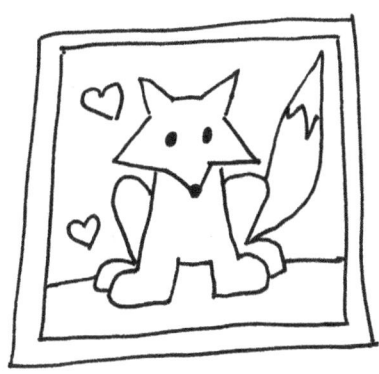

WARNING!!!!

Please put a protection sheet of paper between the pages when using markers to prevent bleed-through.

A protection sheet is included at the back of this book.

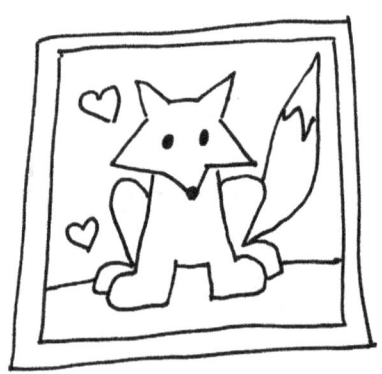

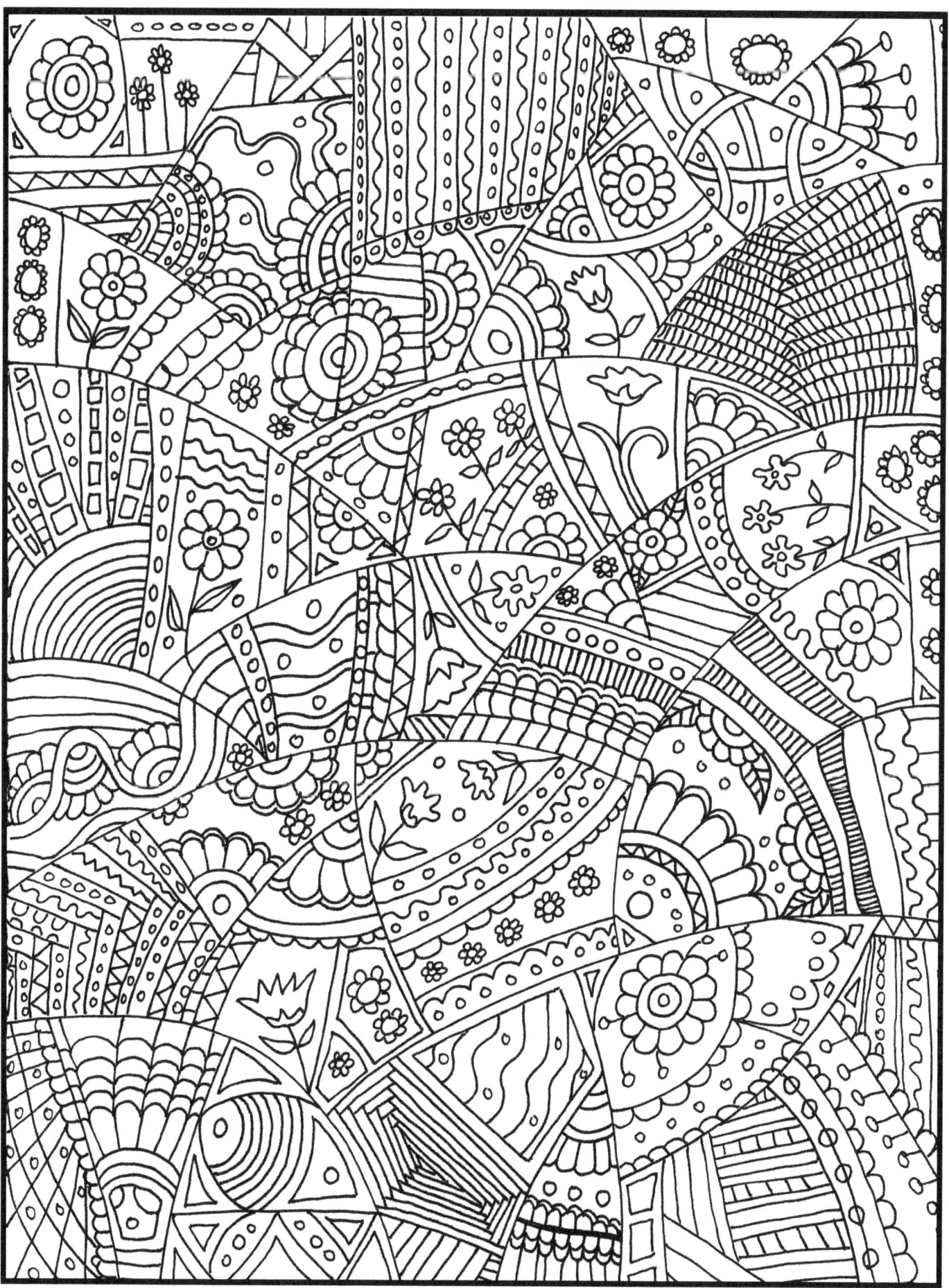

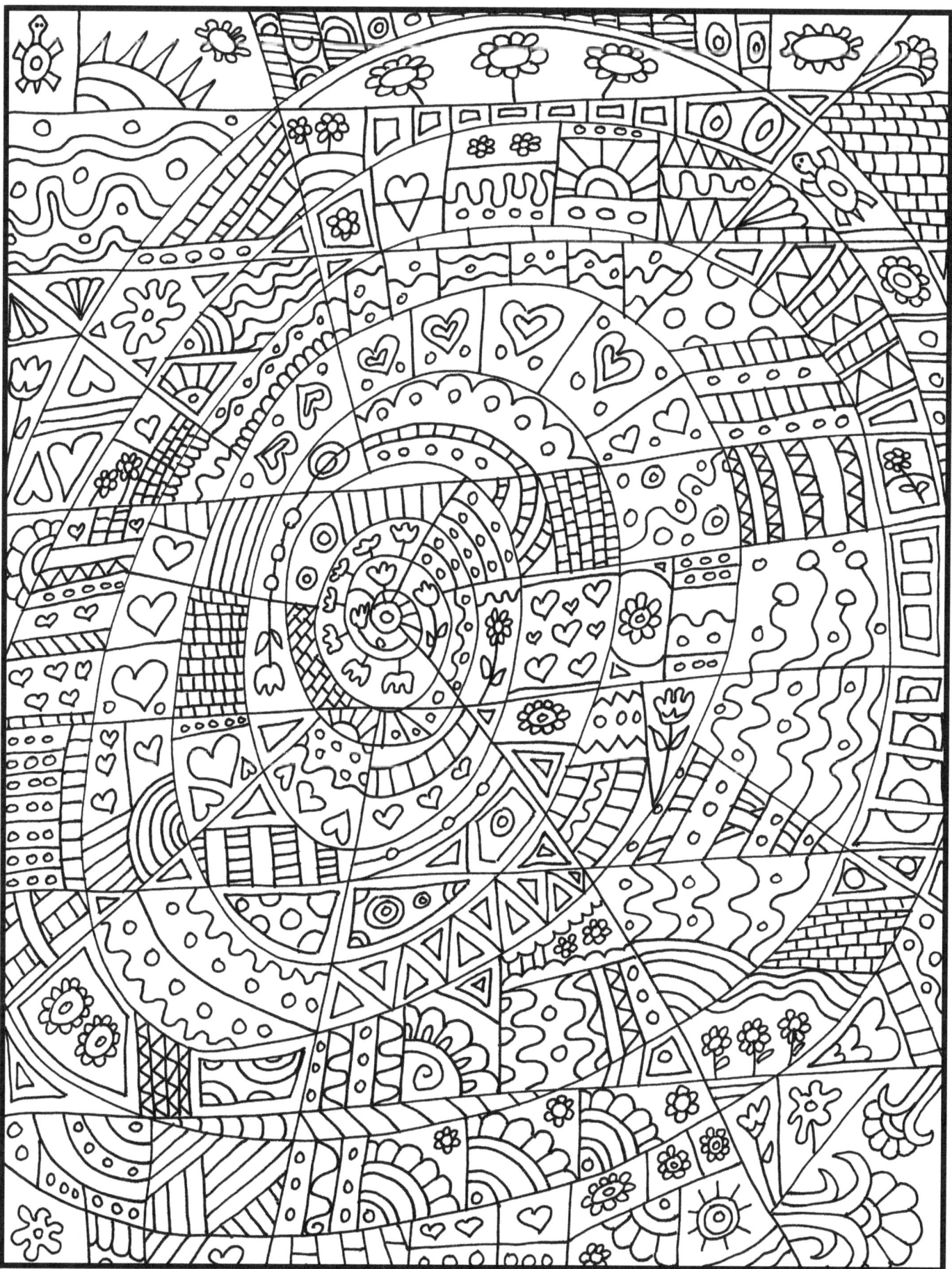

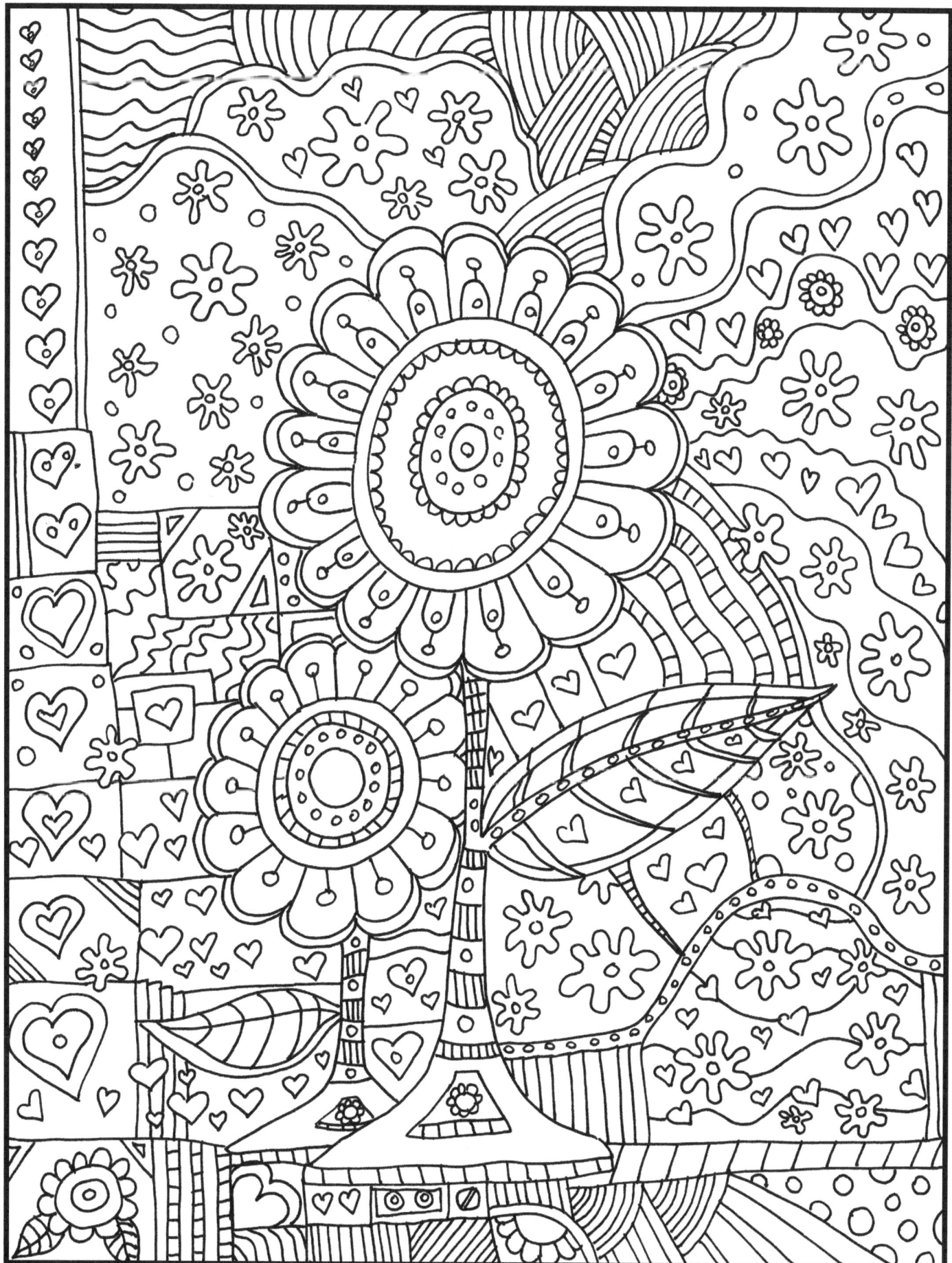

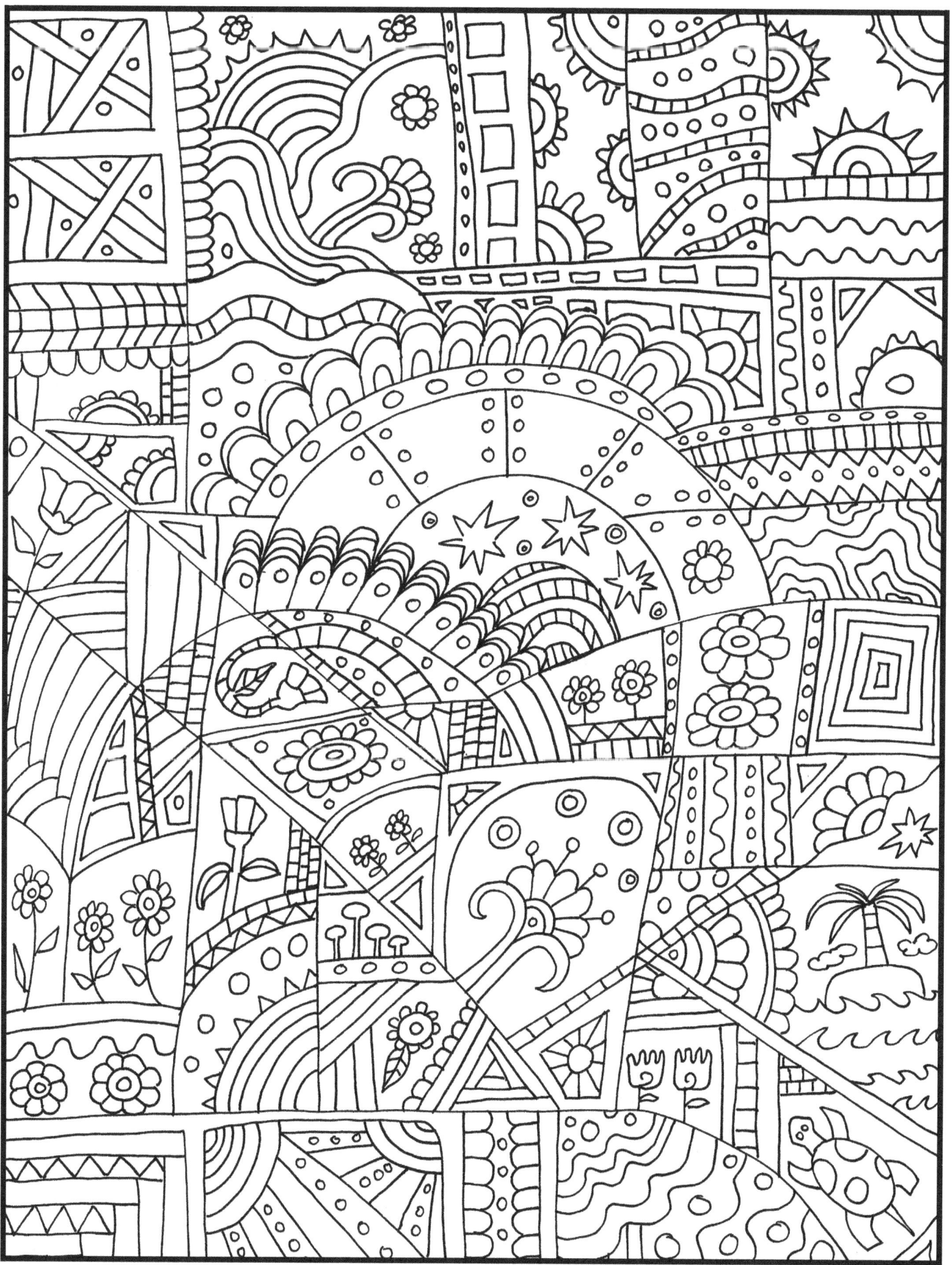

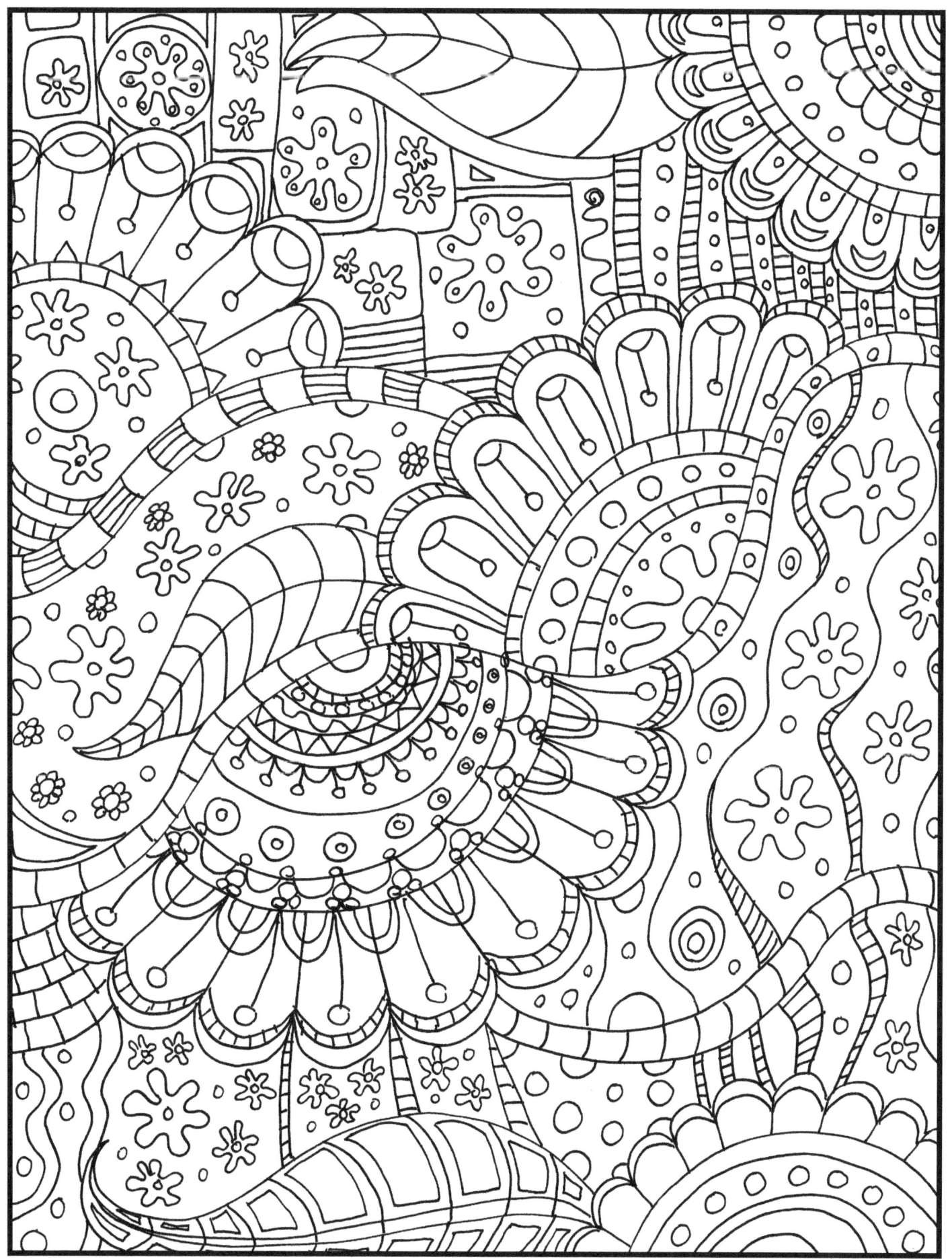

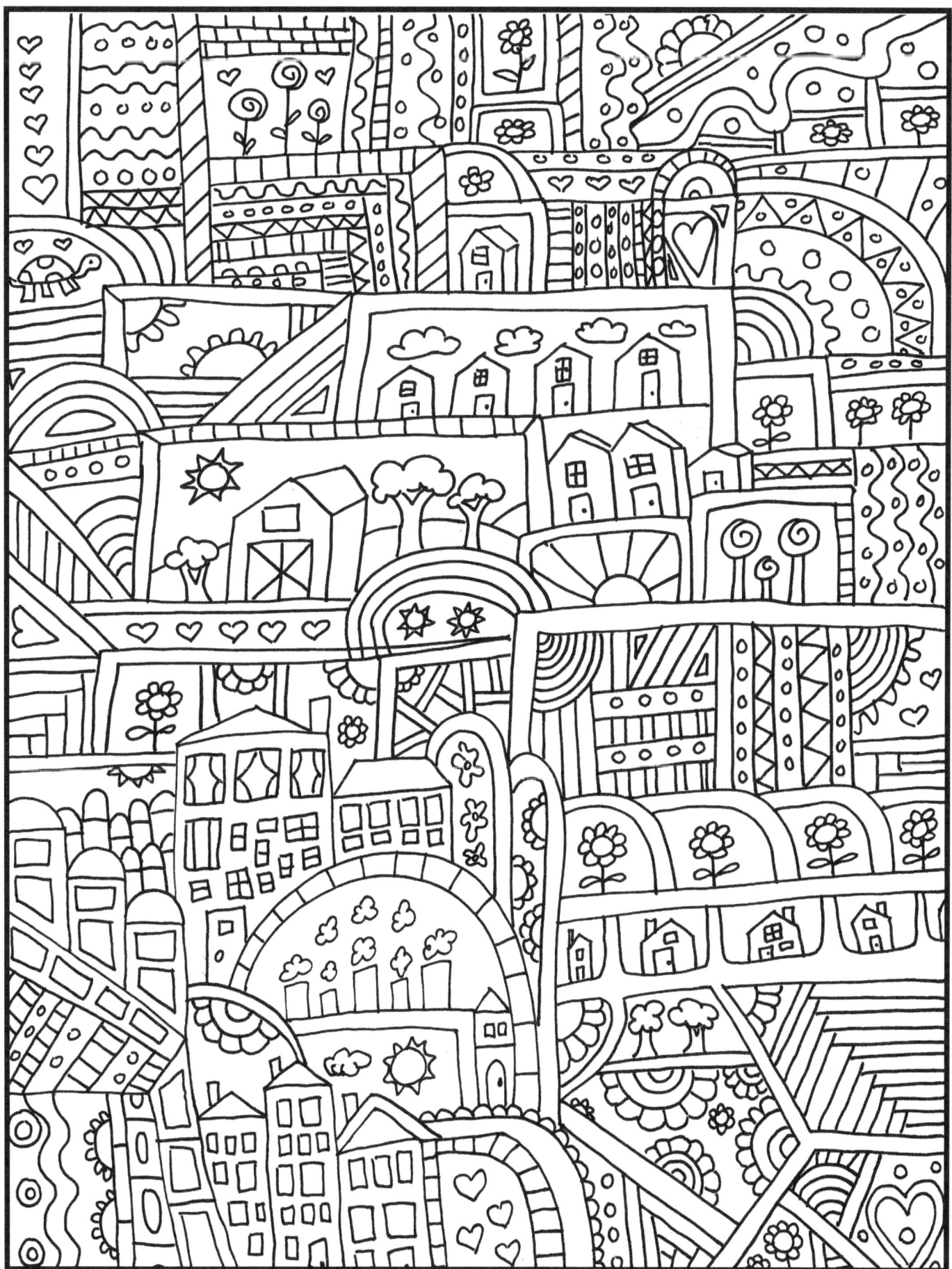

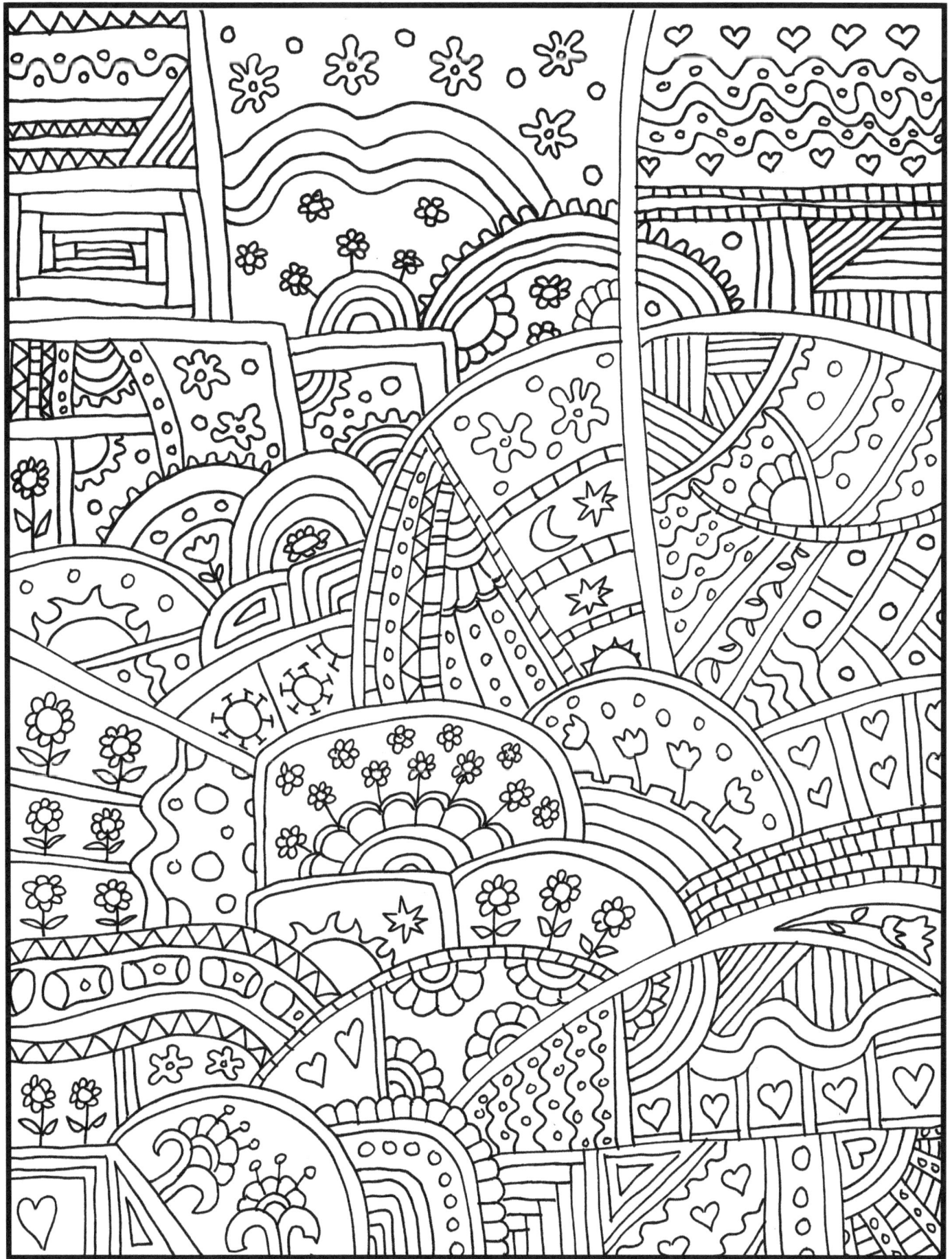

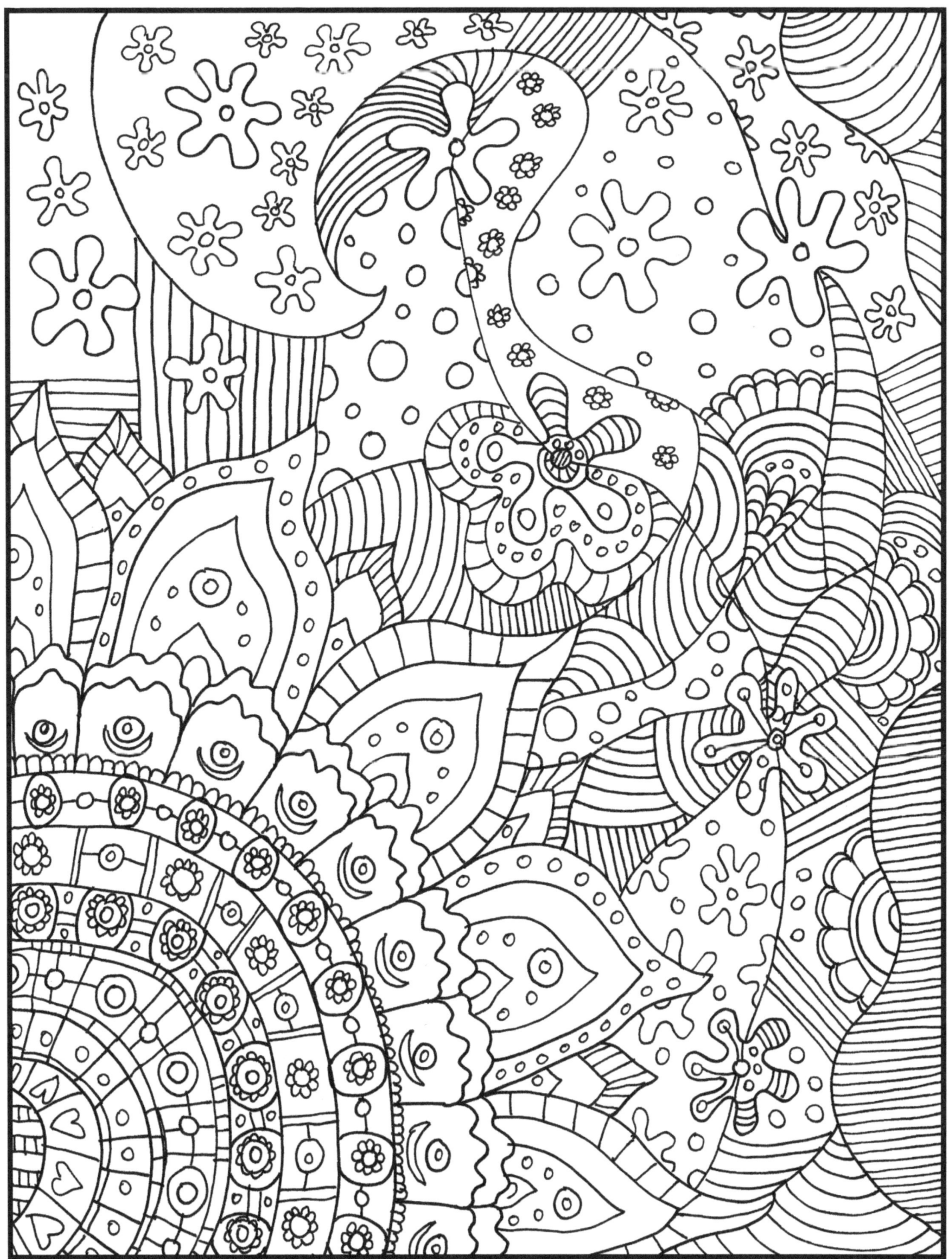

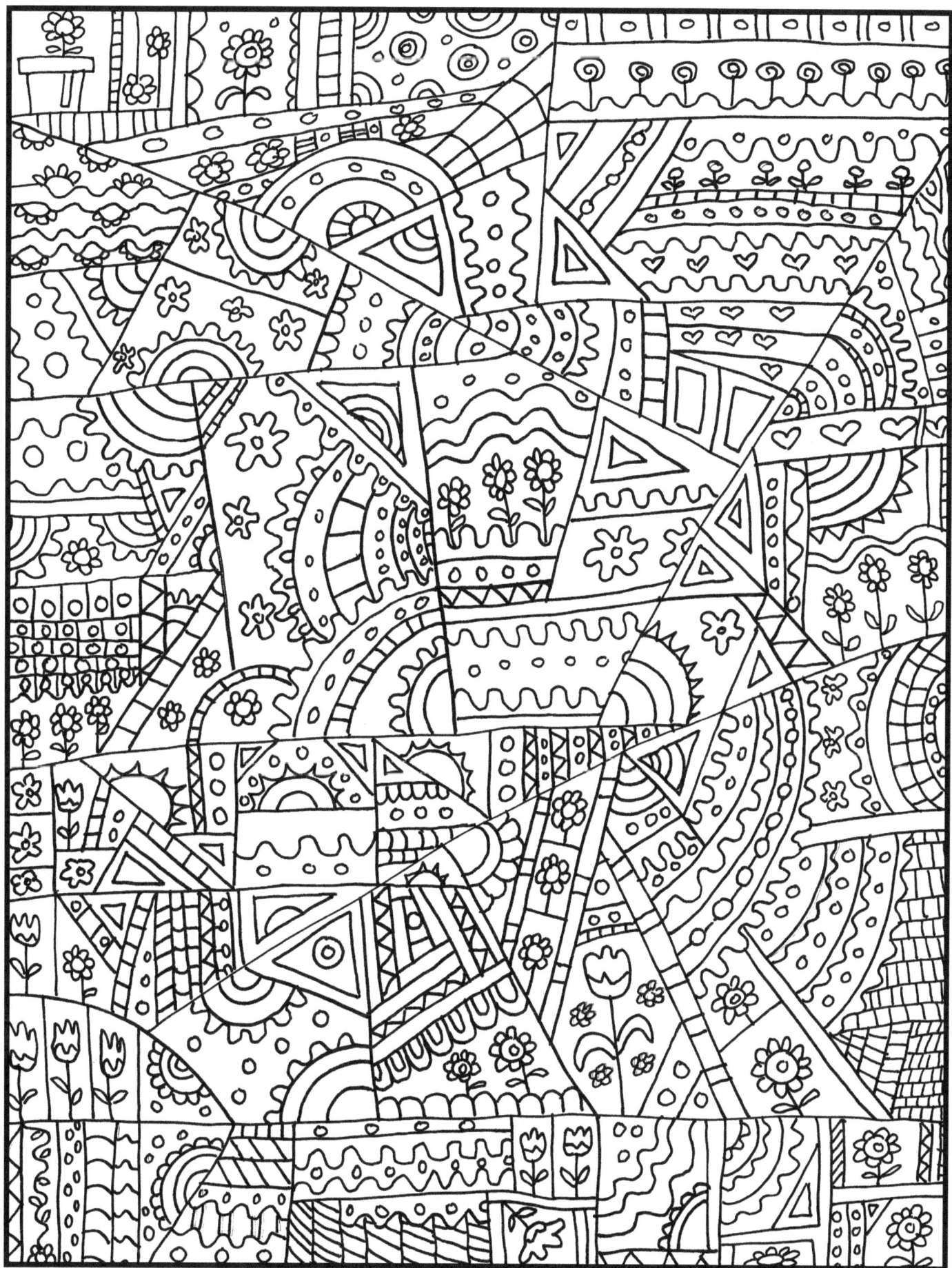

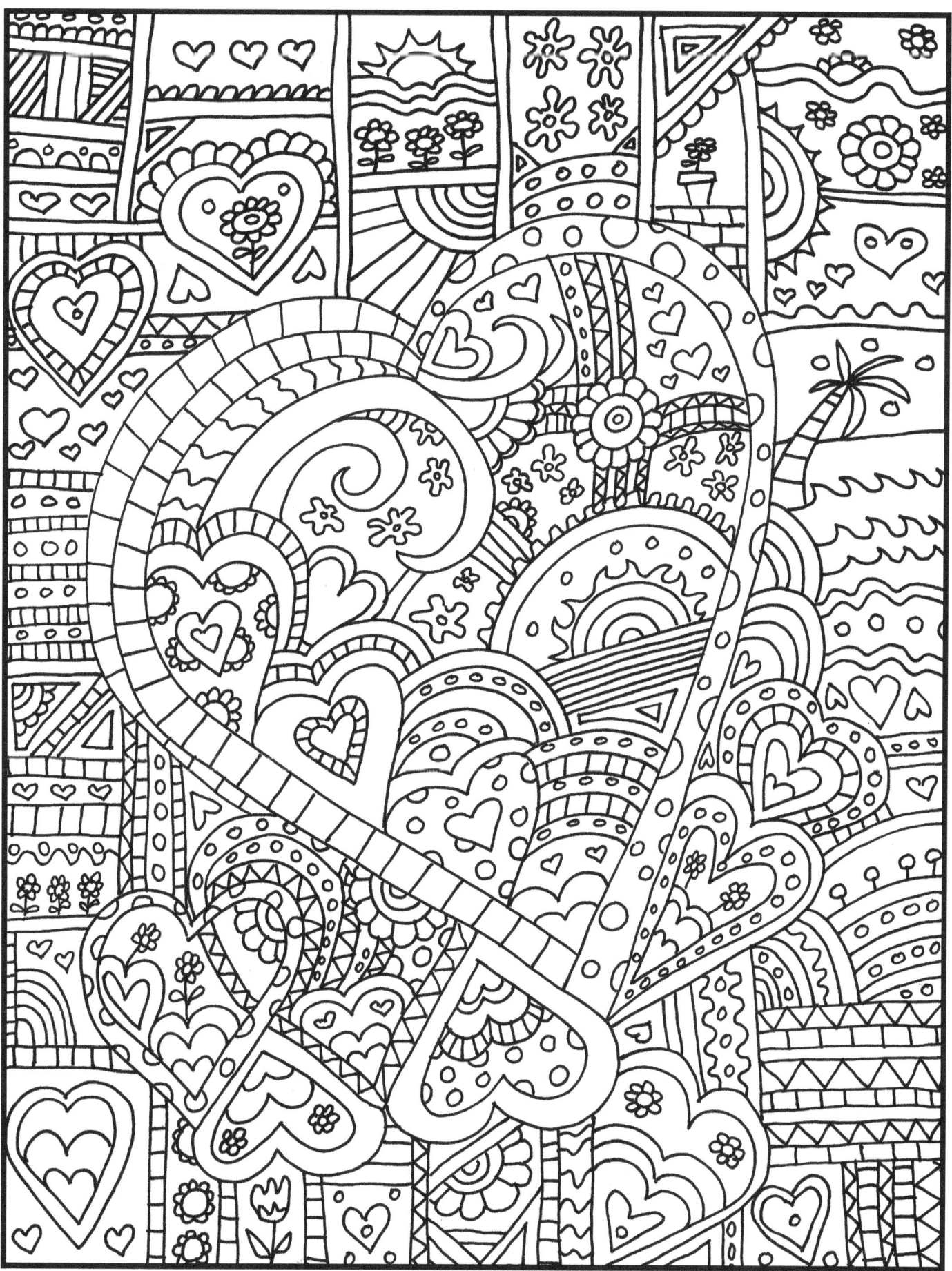

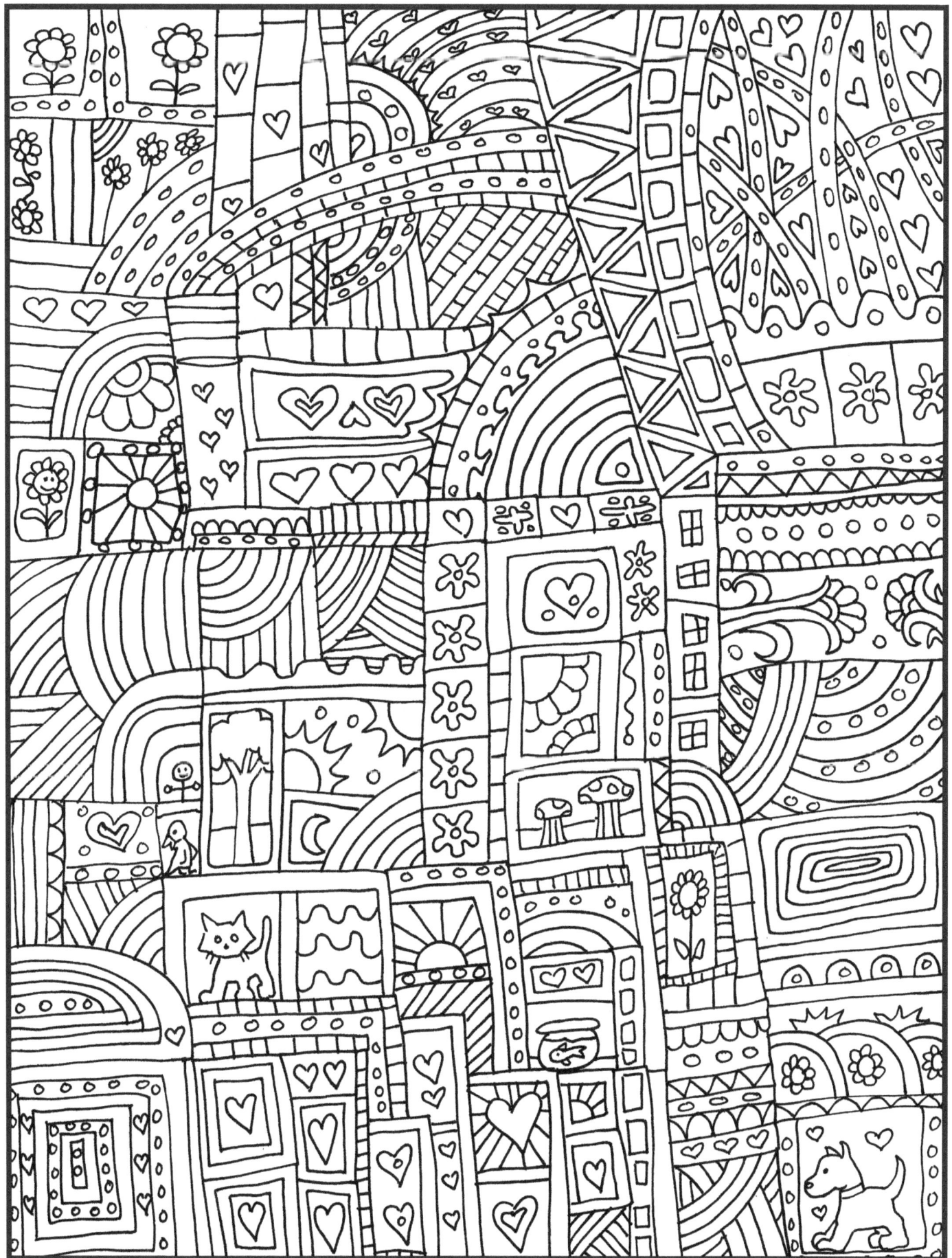

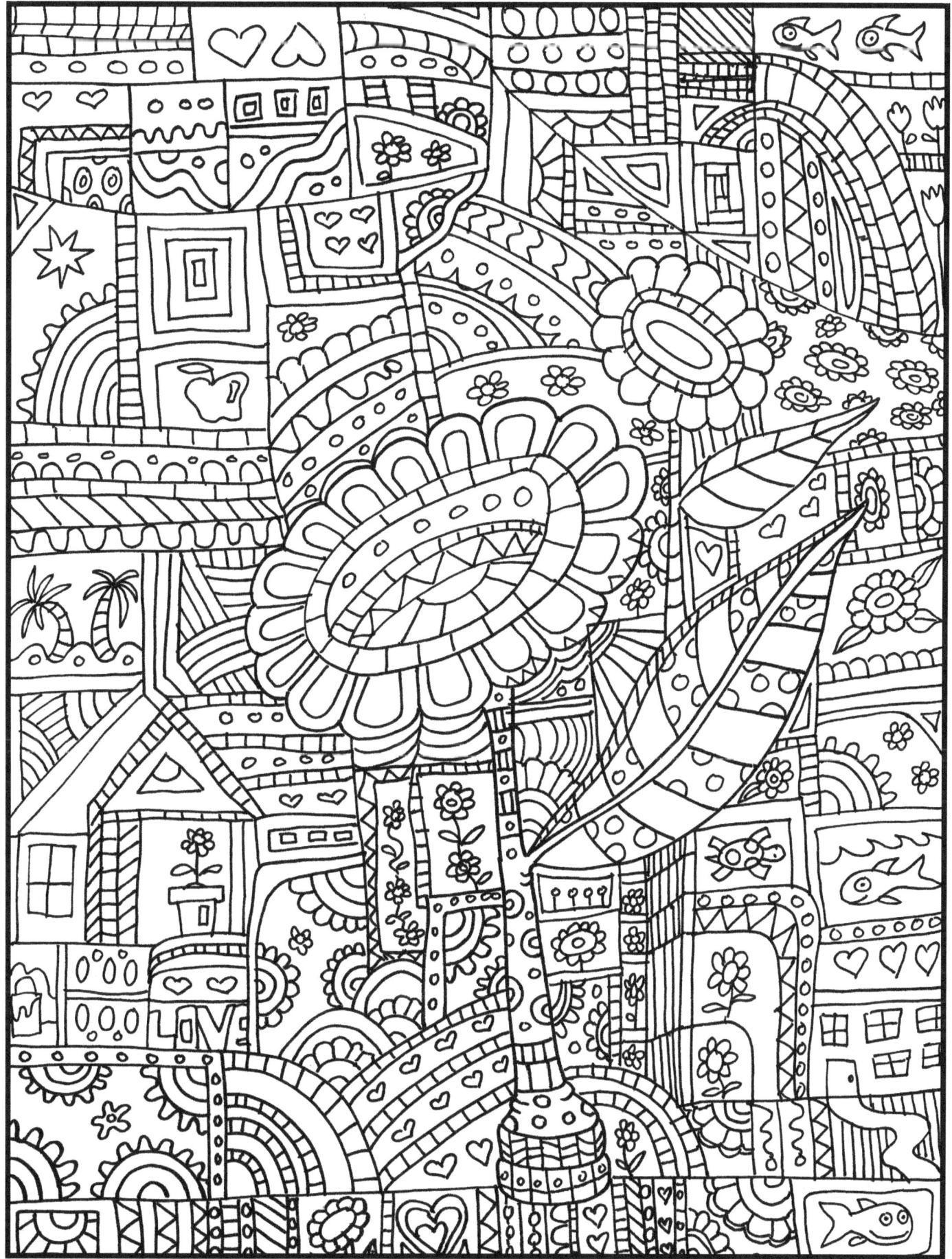

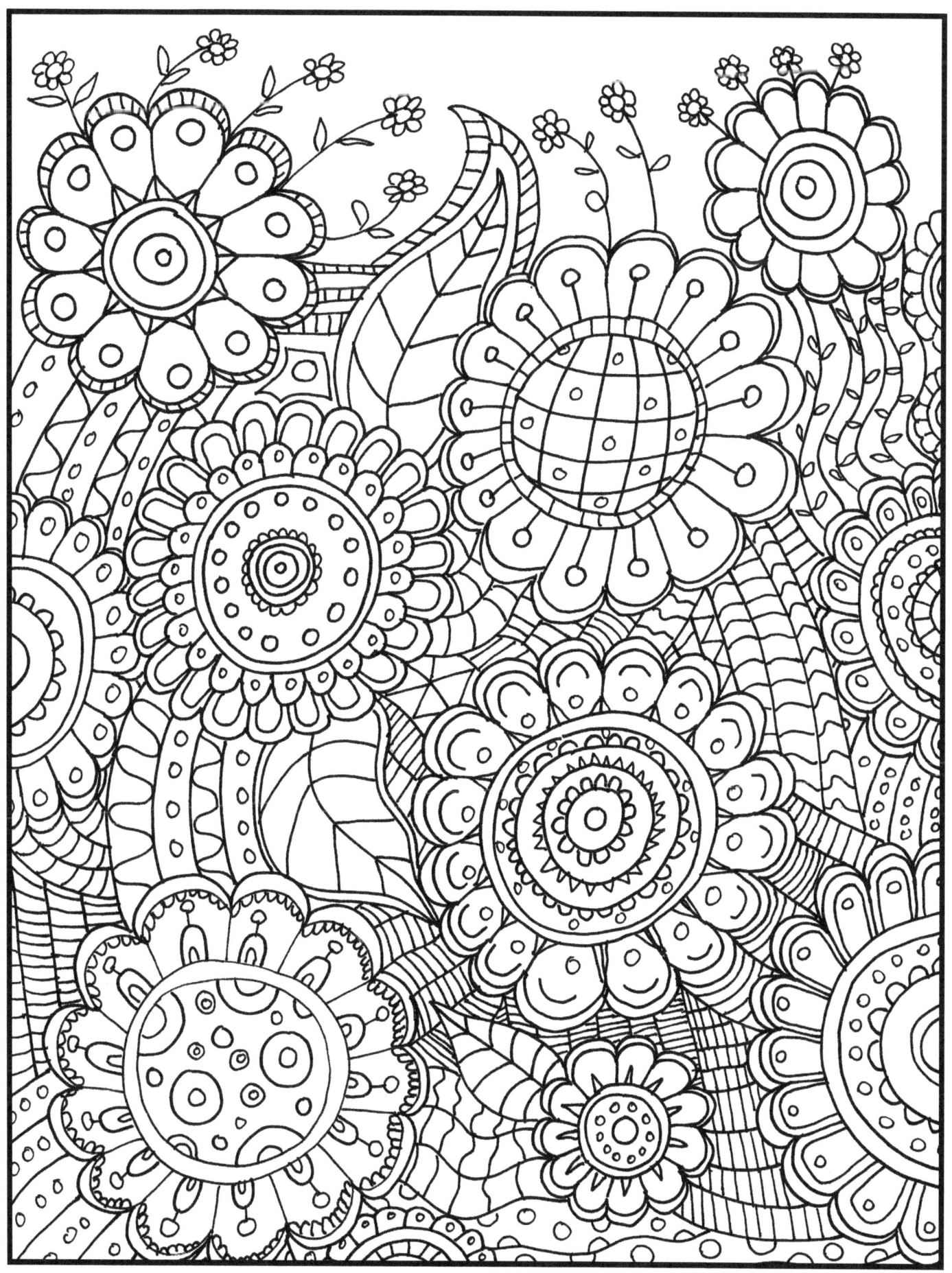

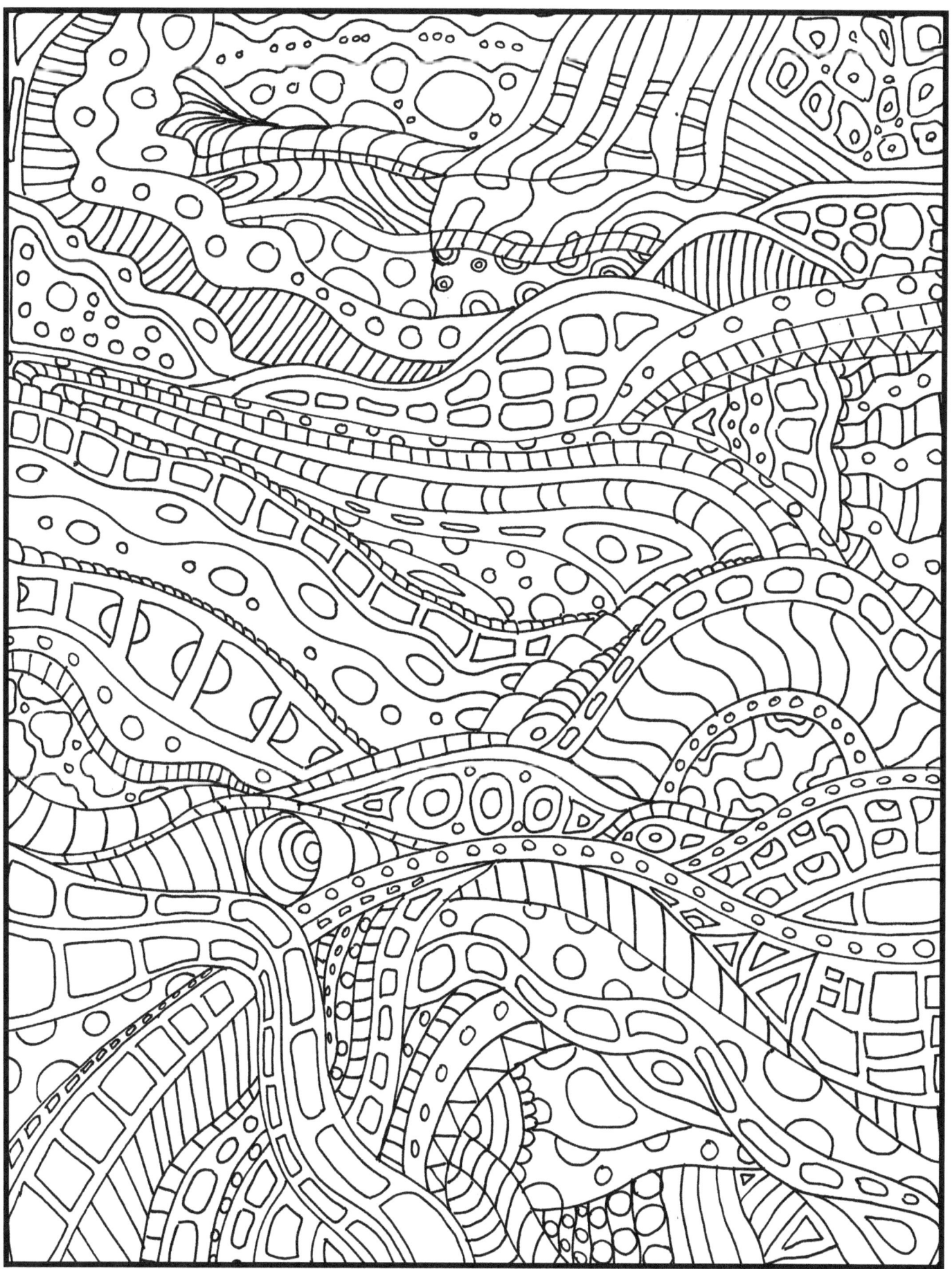

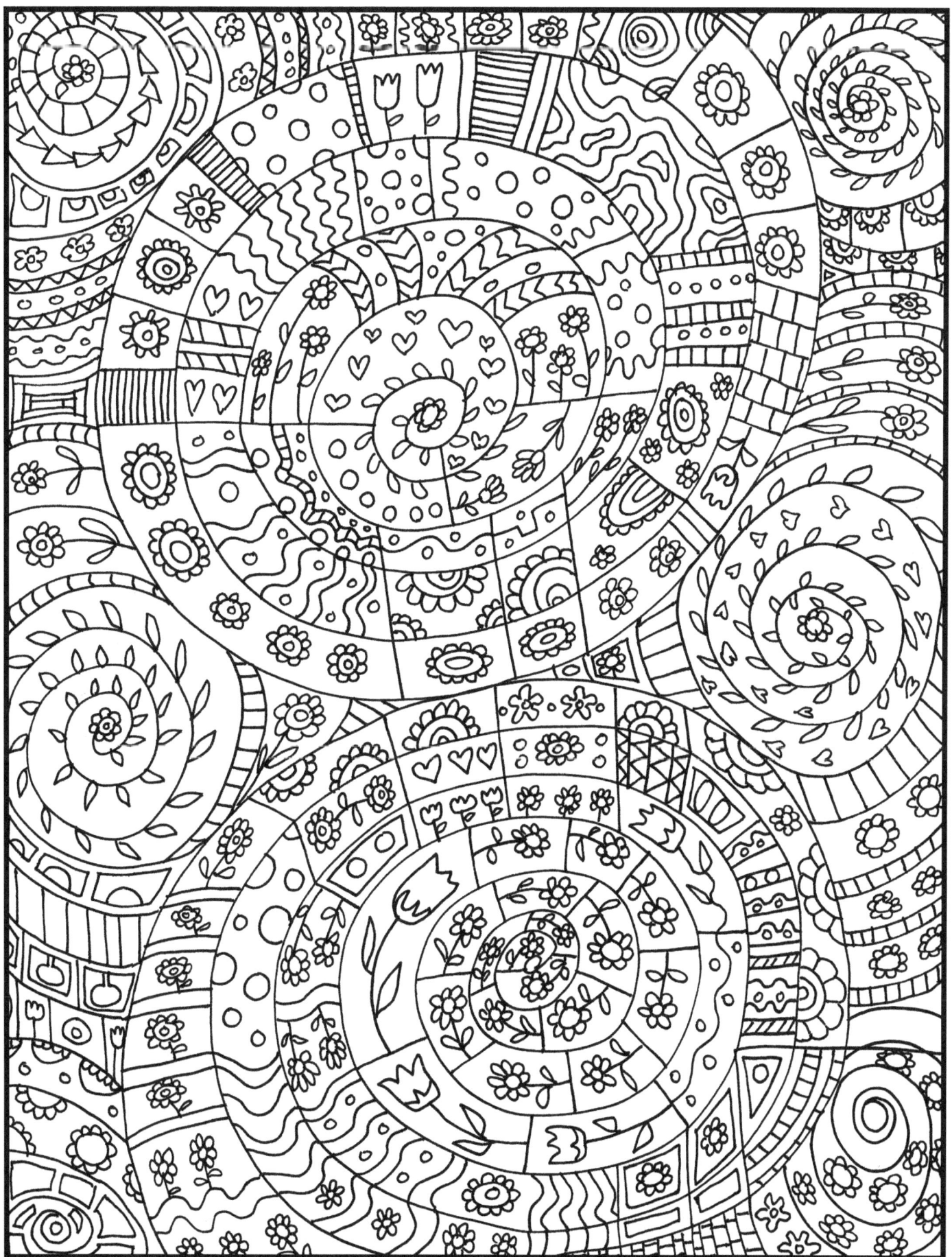

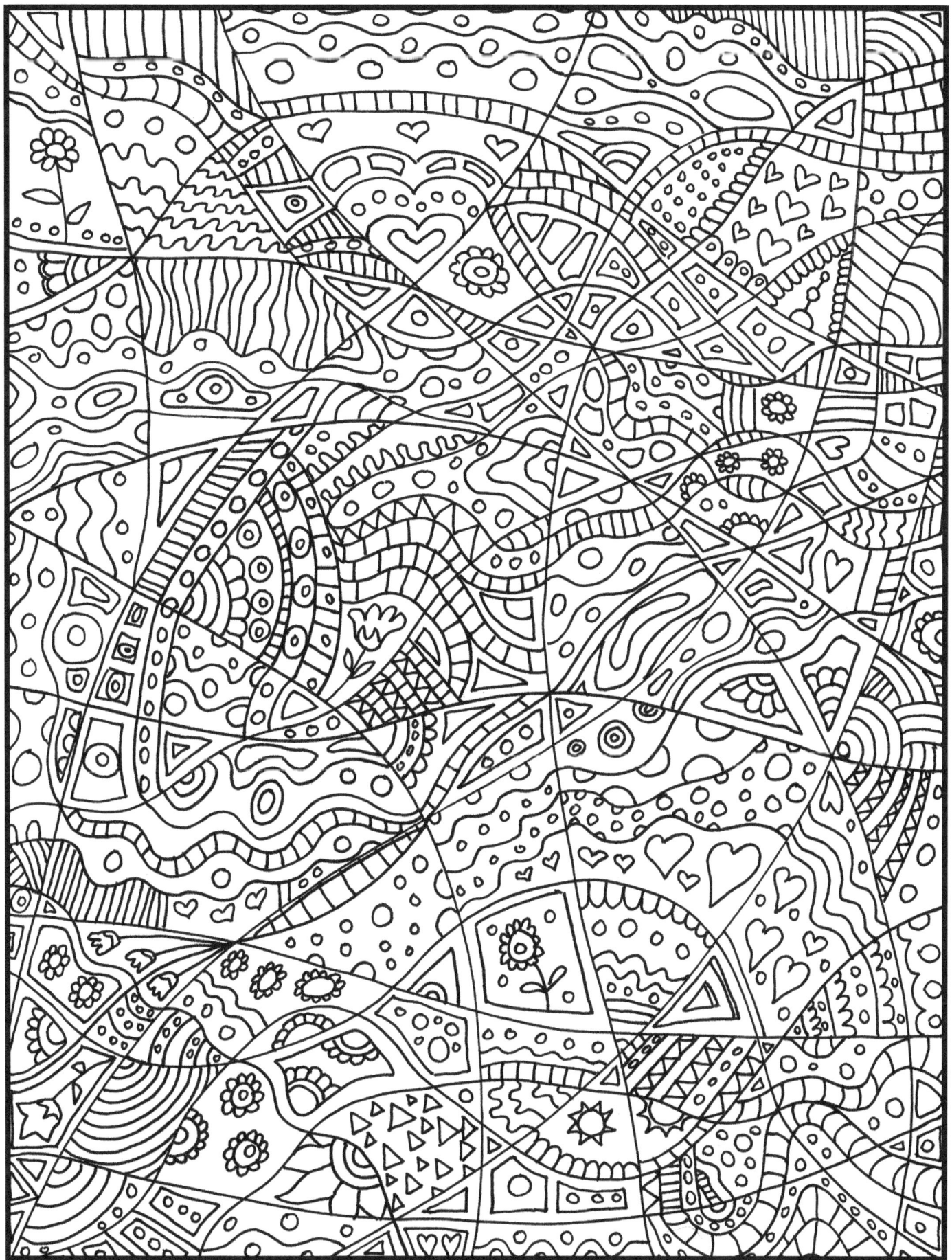

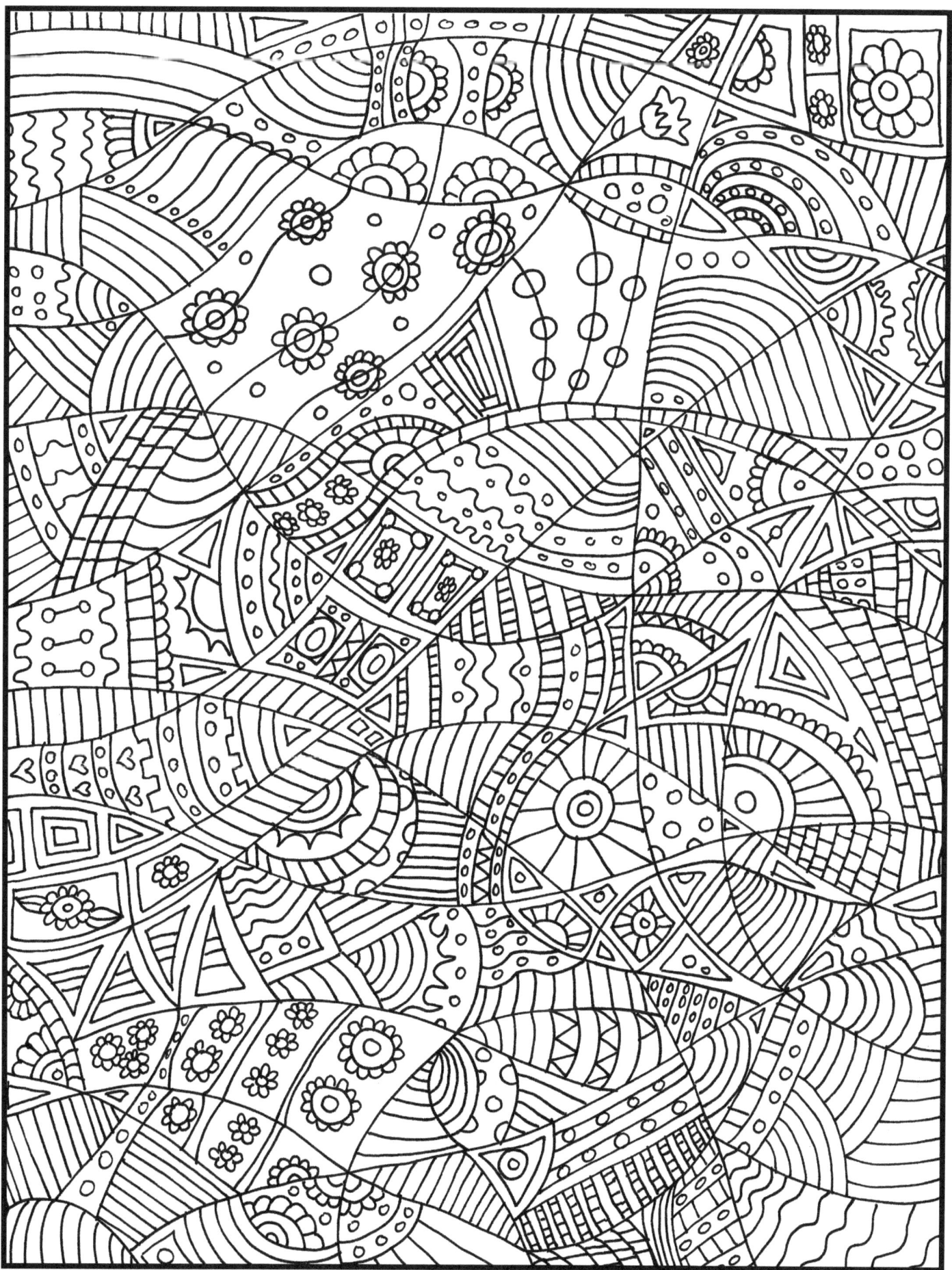

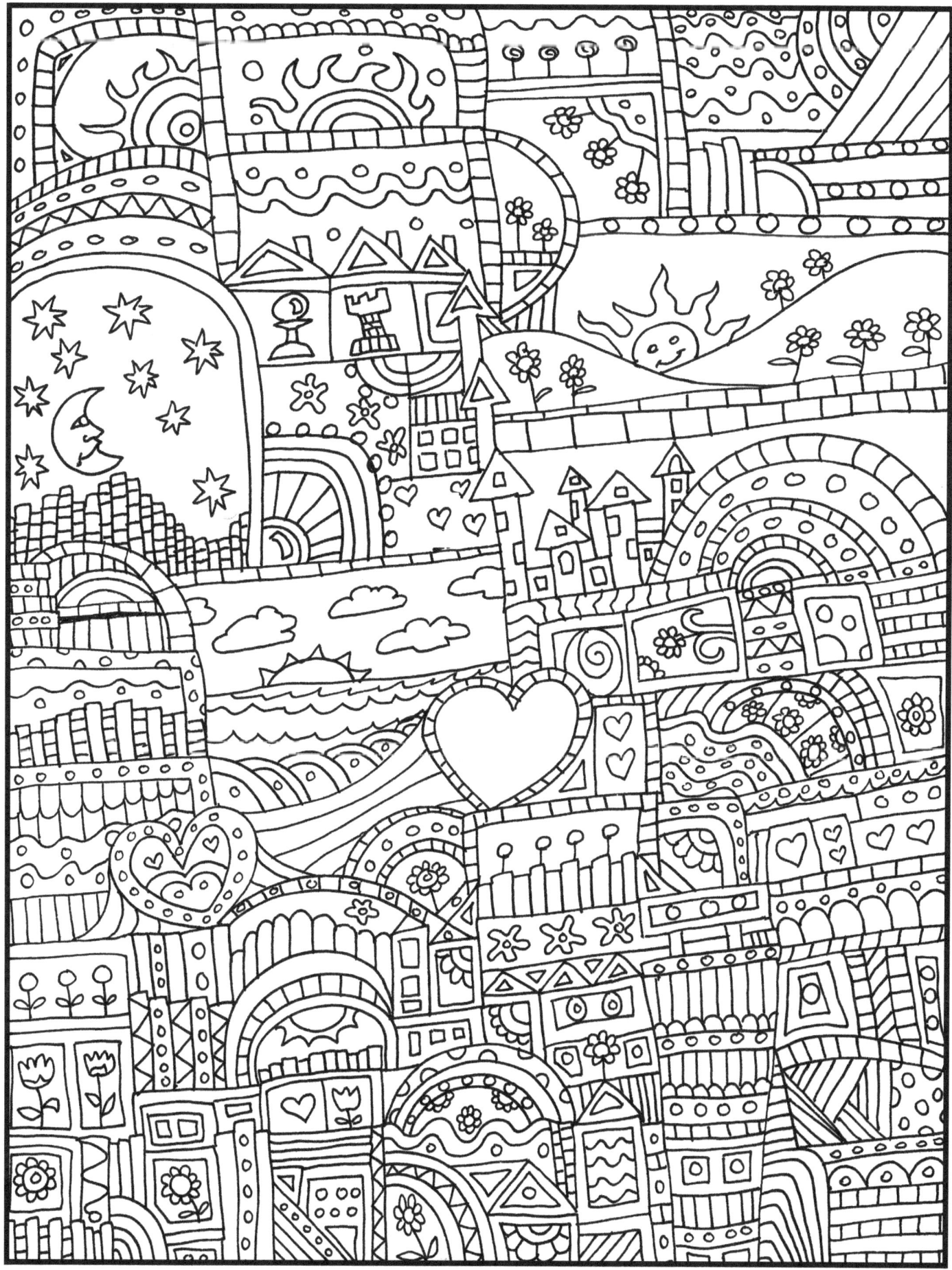

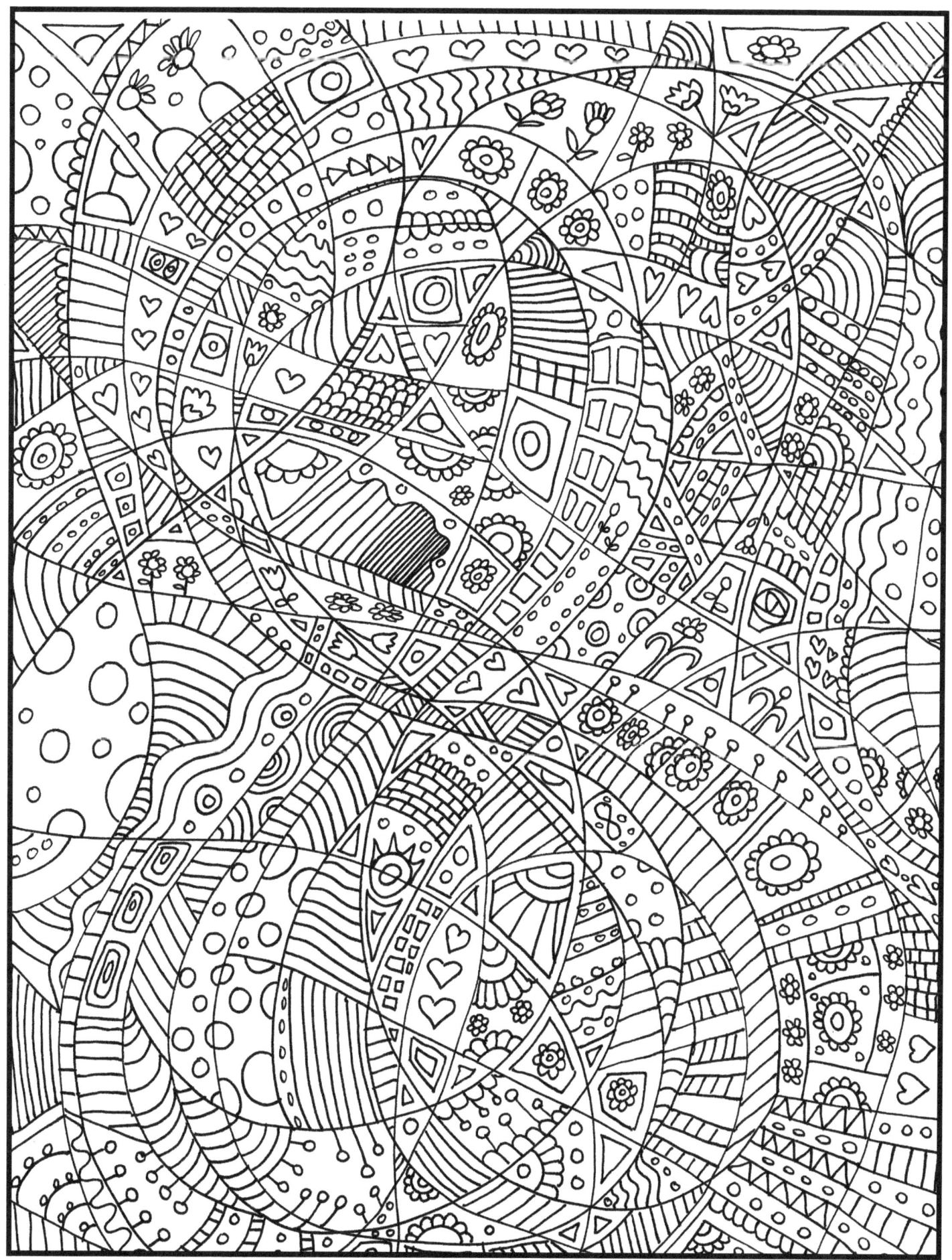

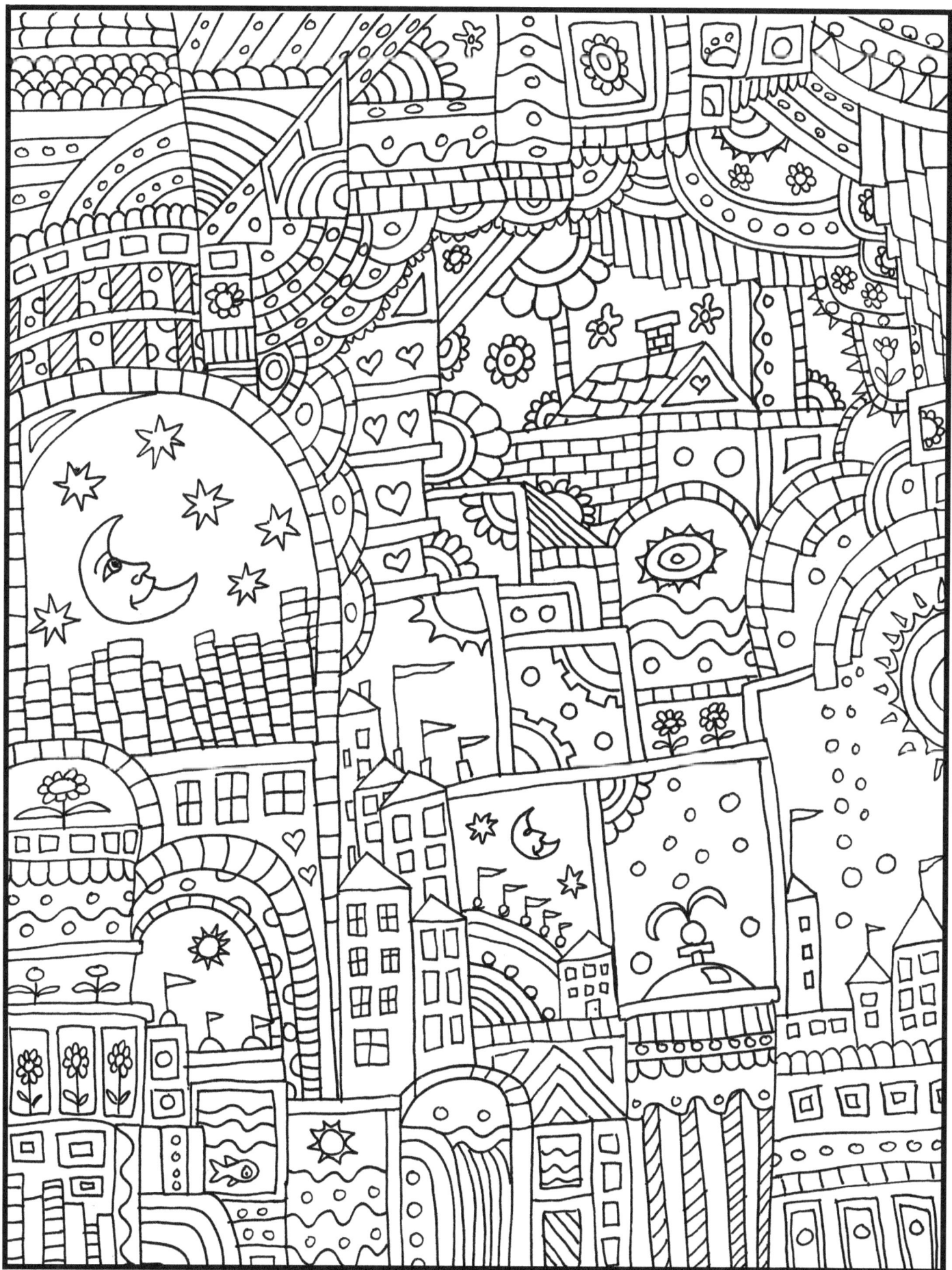

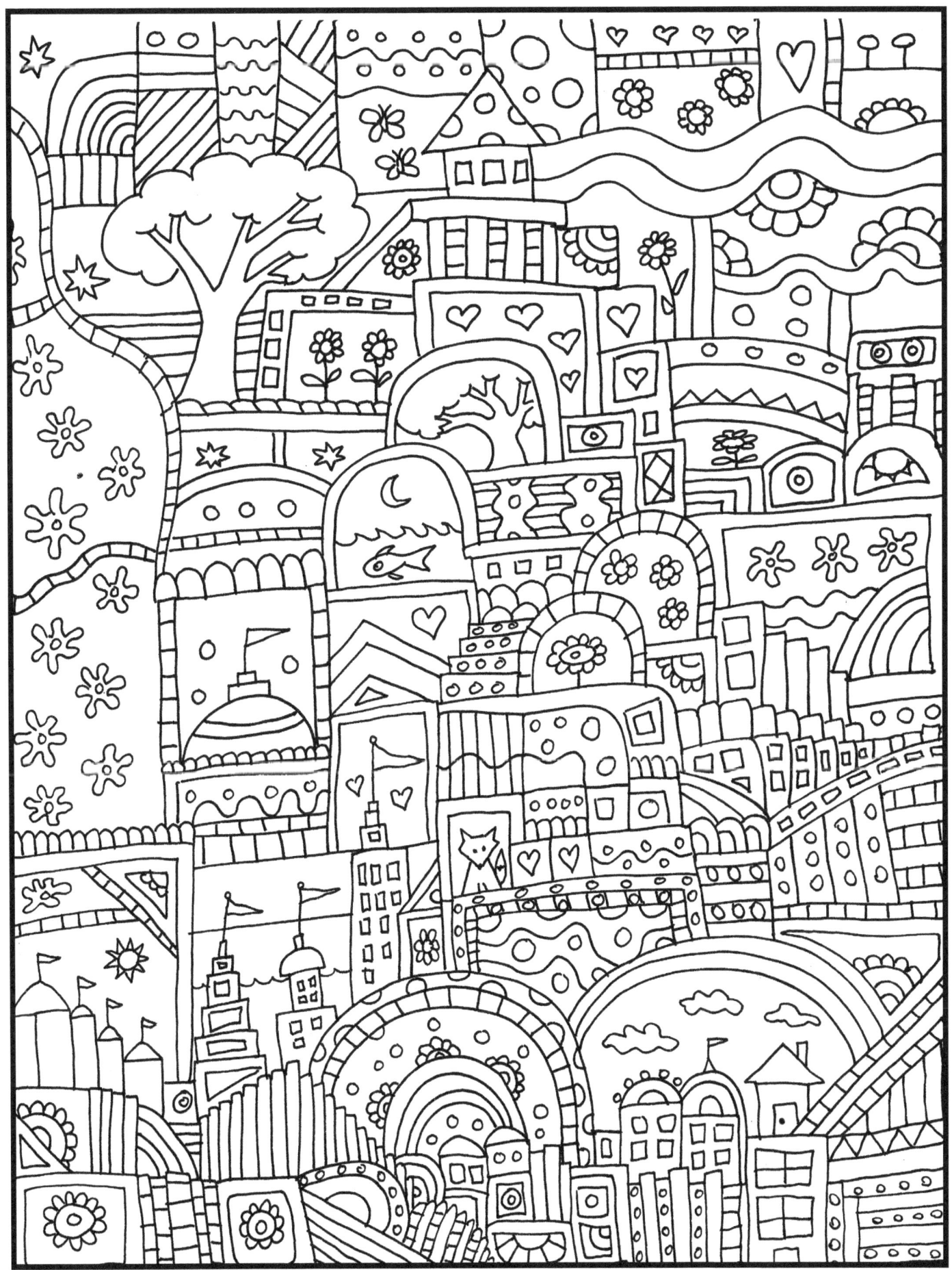

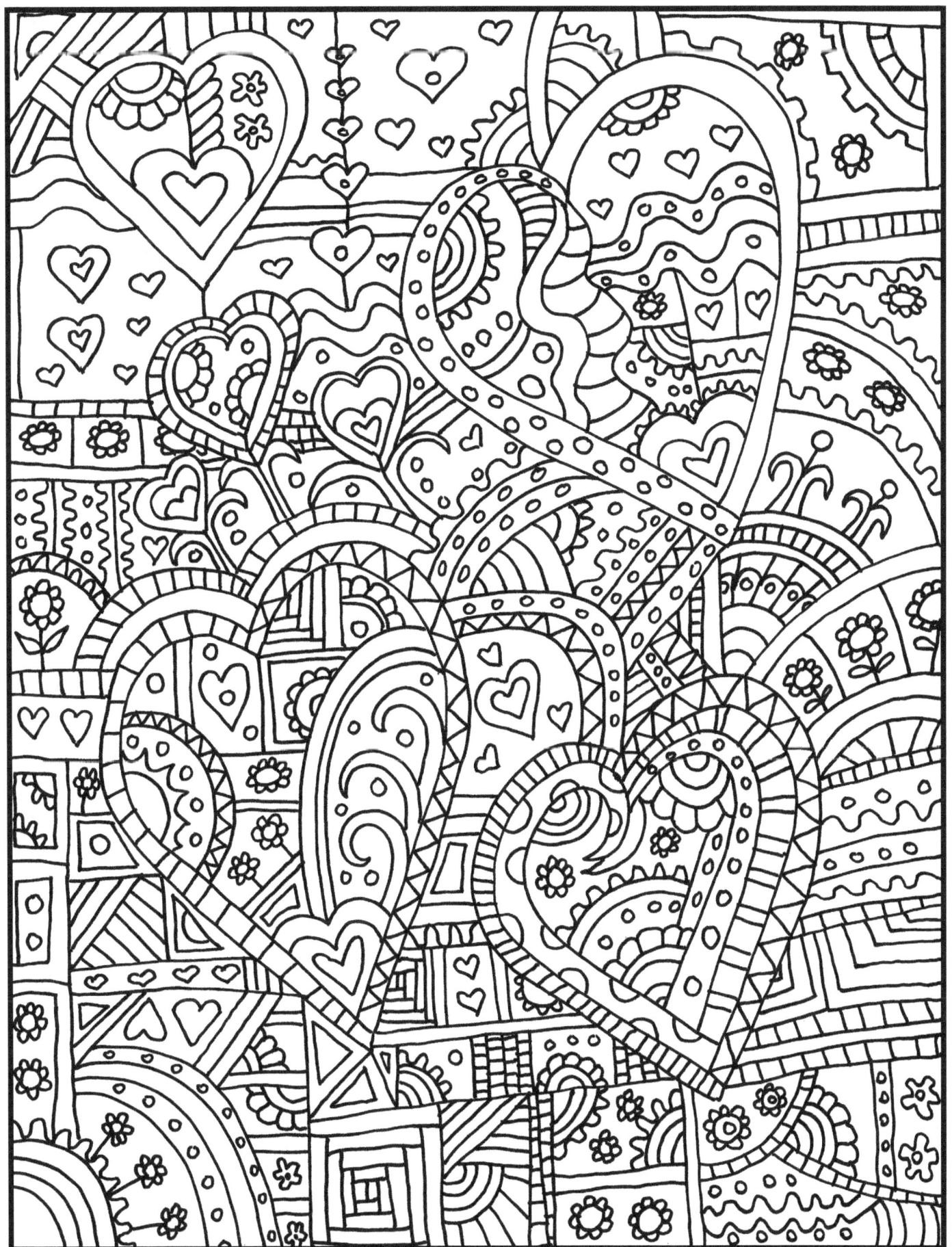

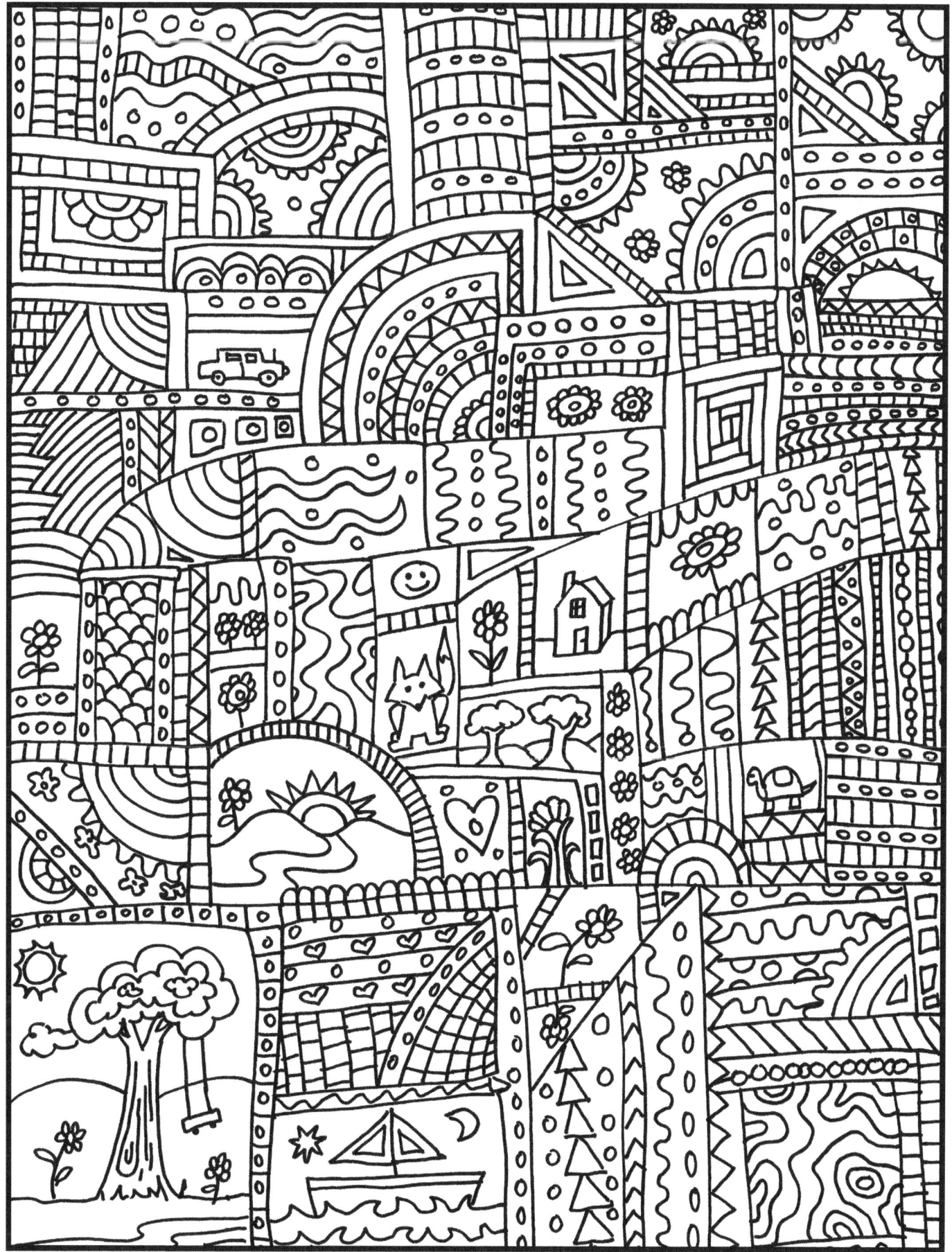

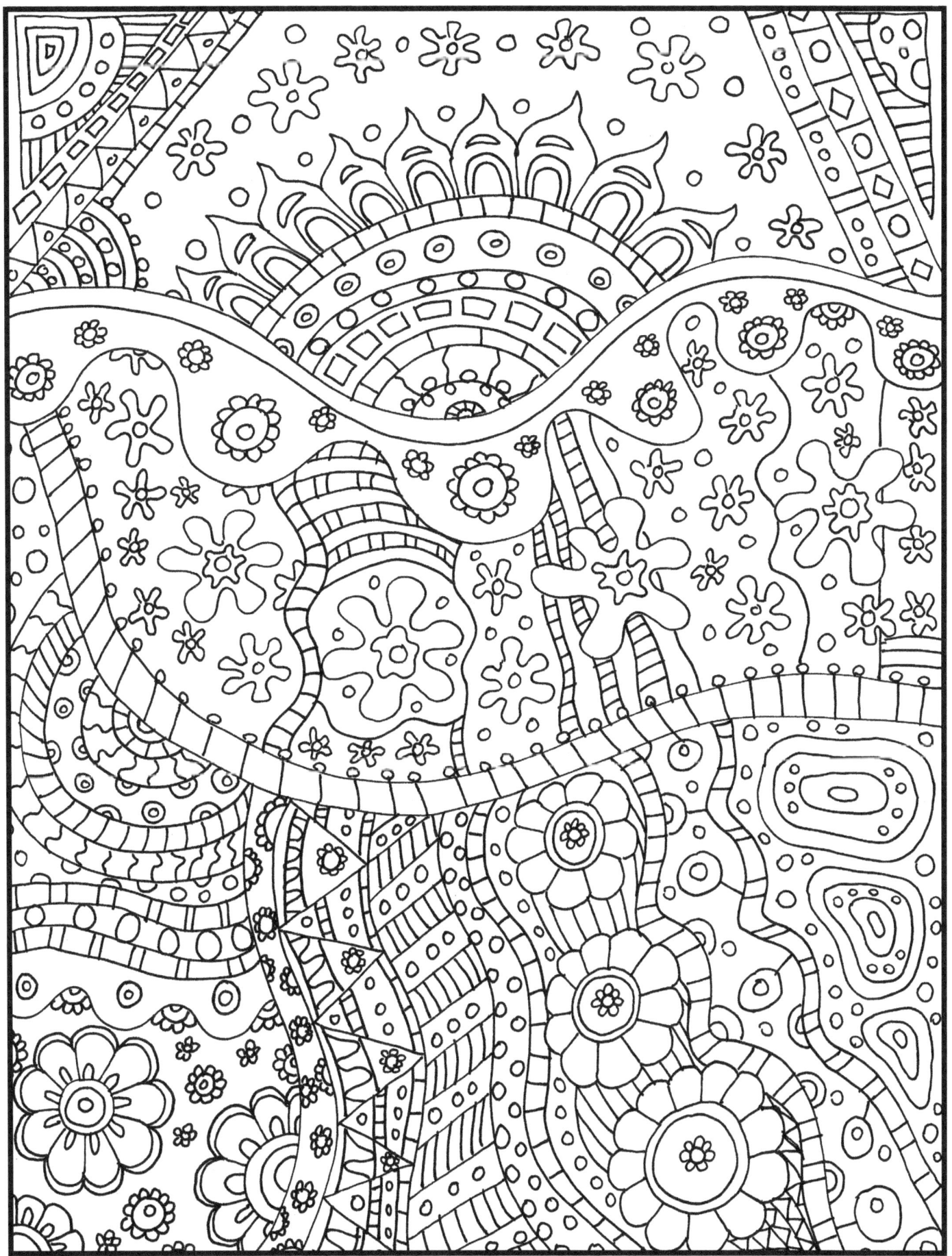

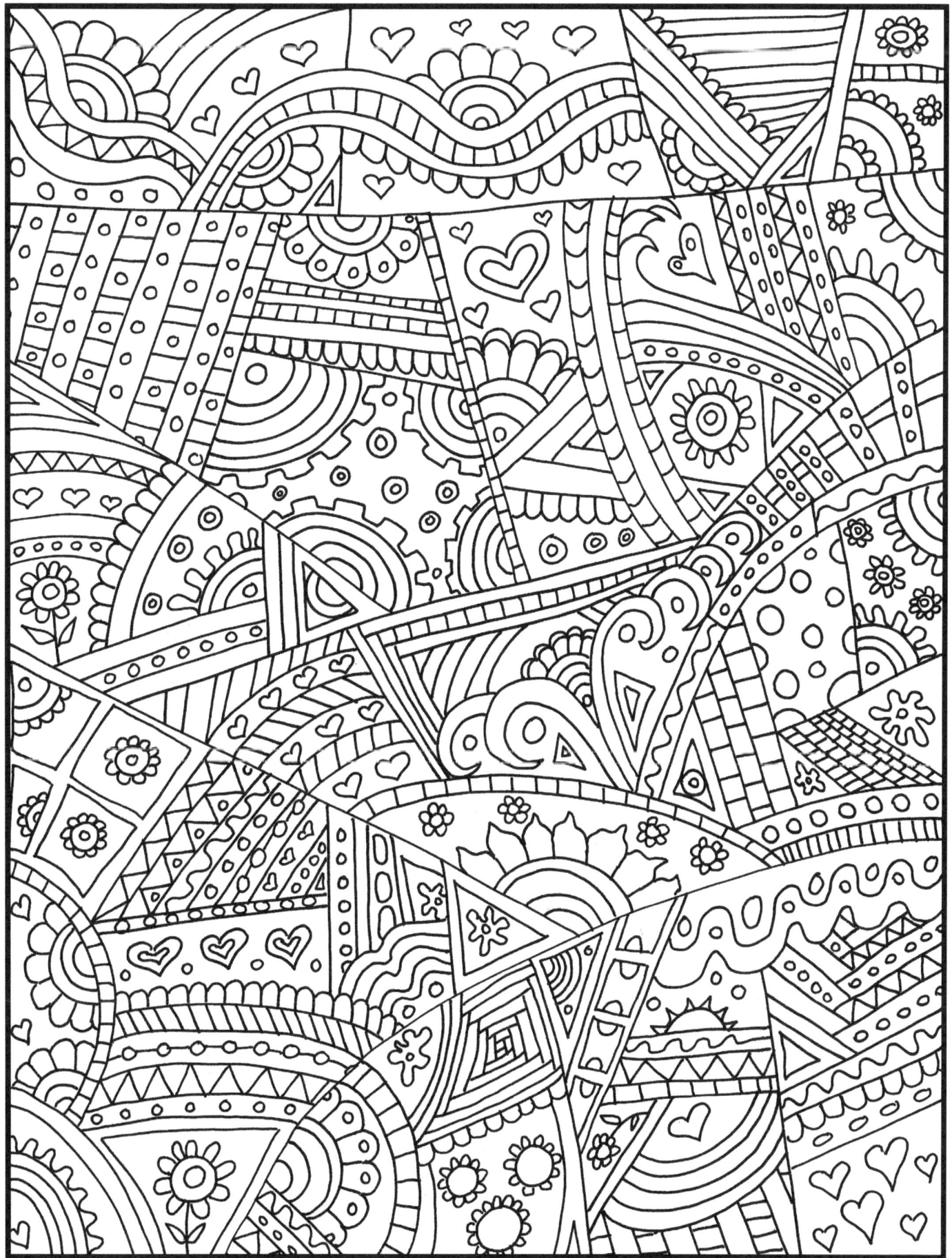

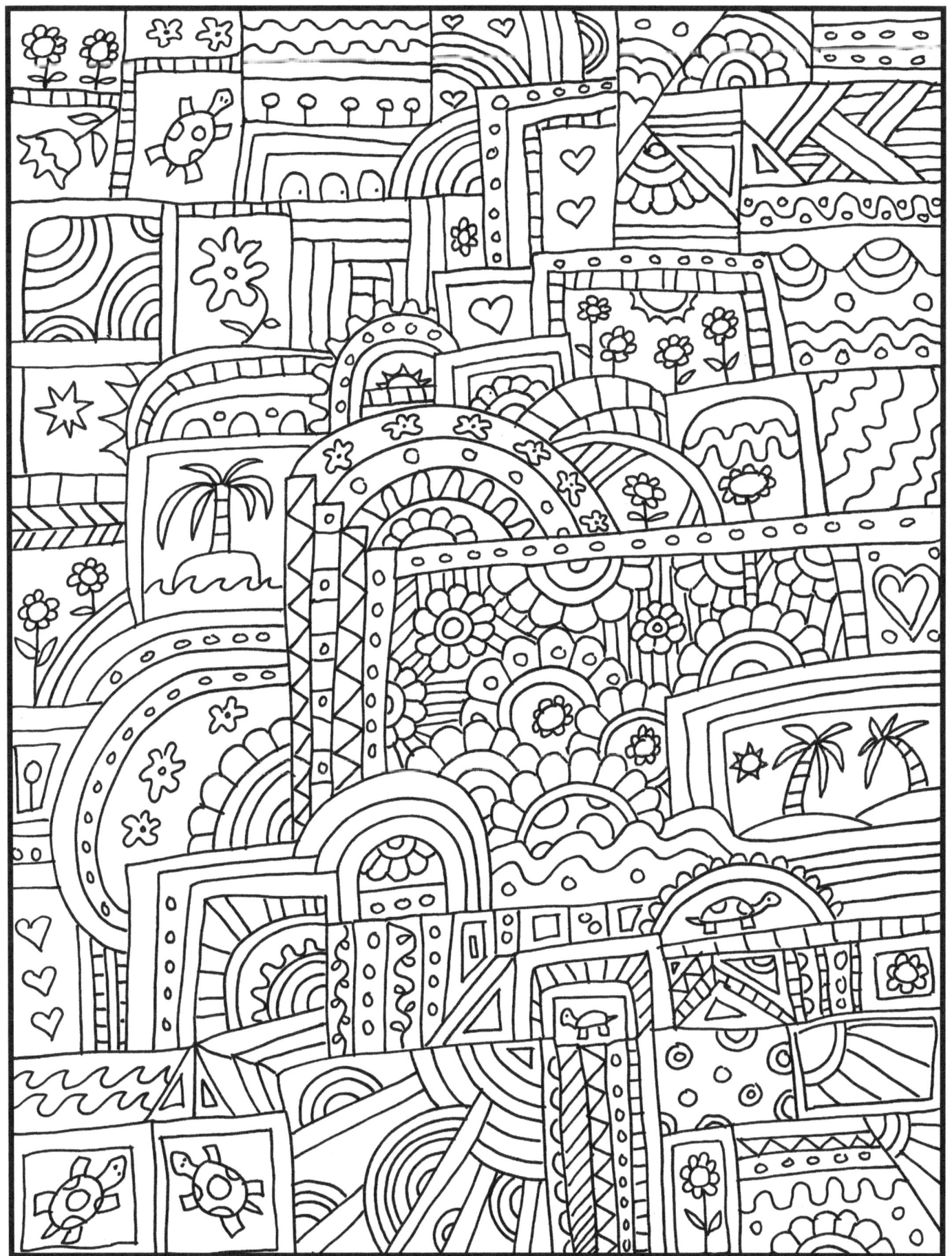

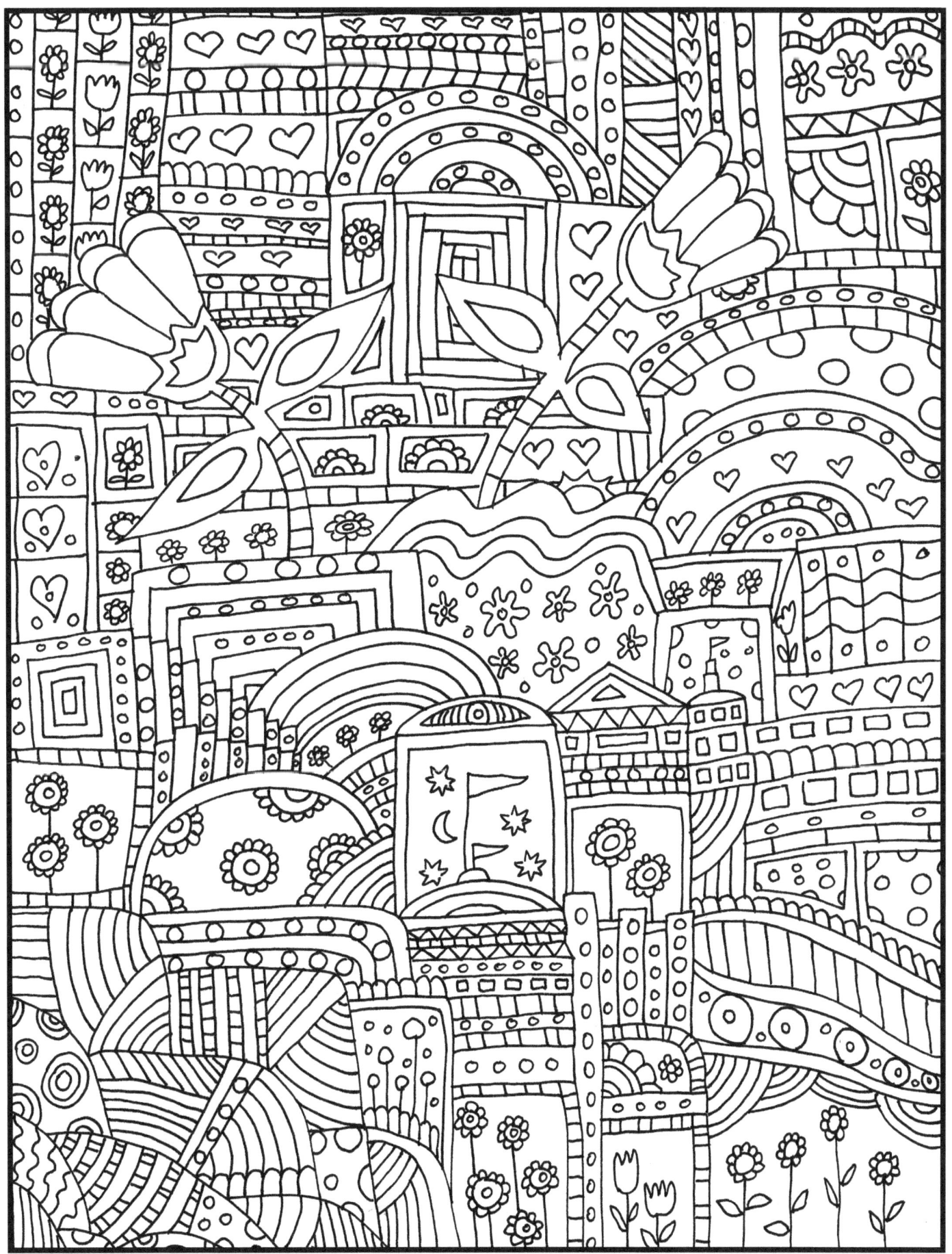

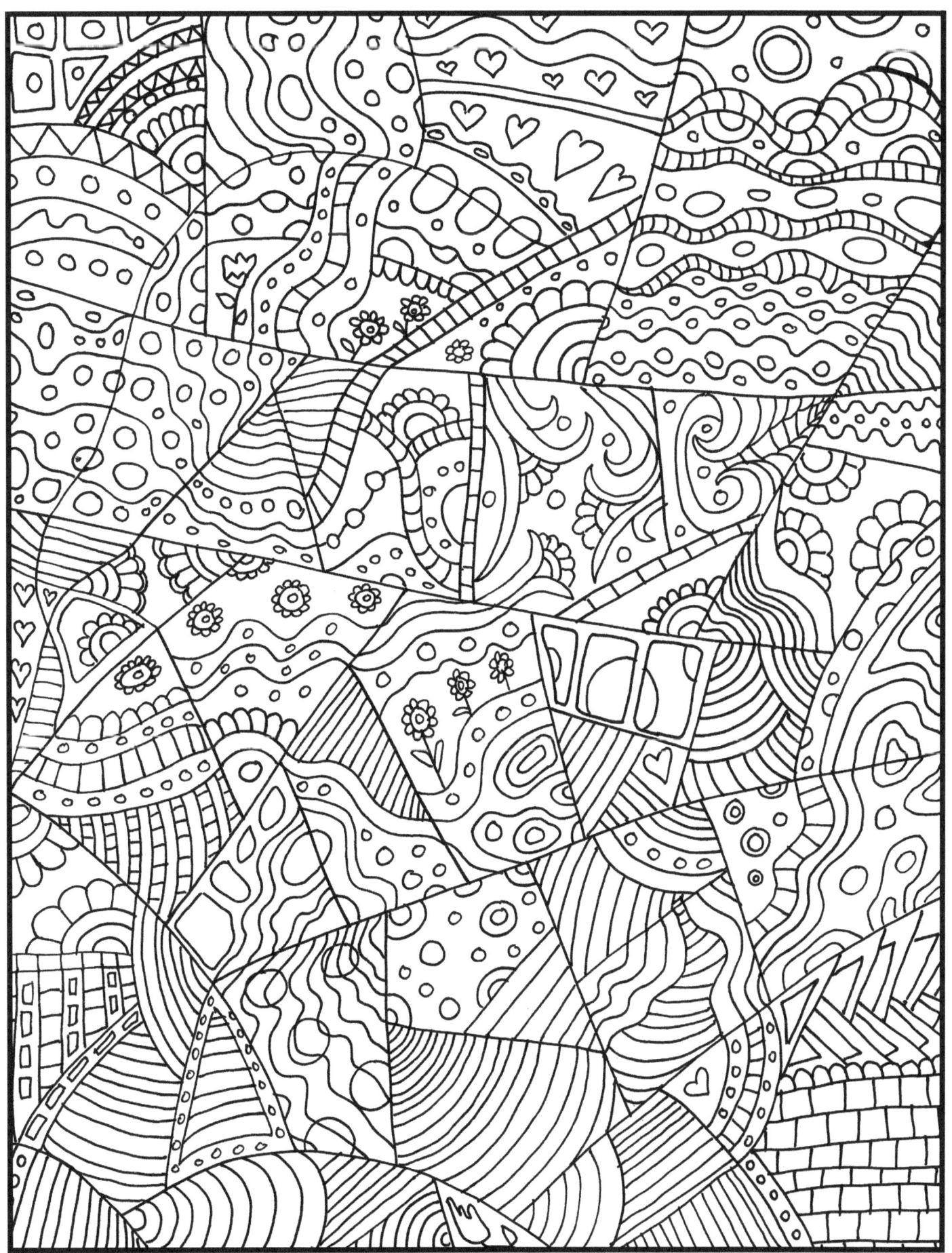

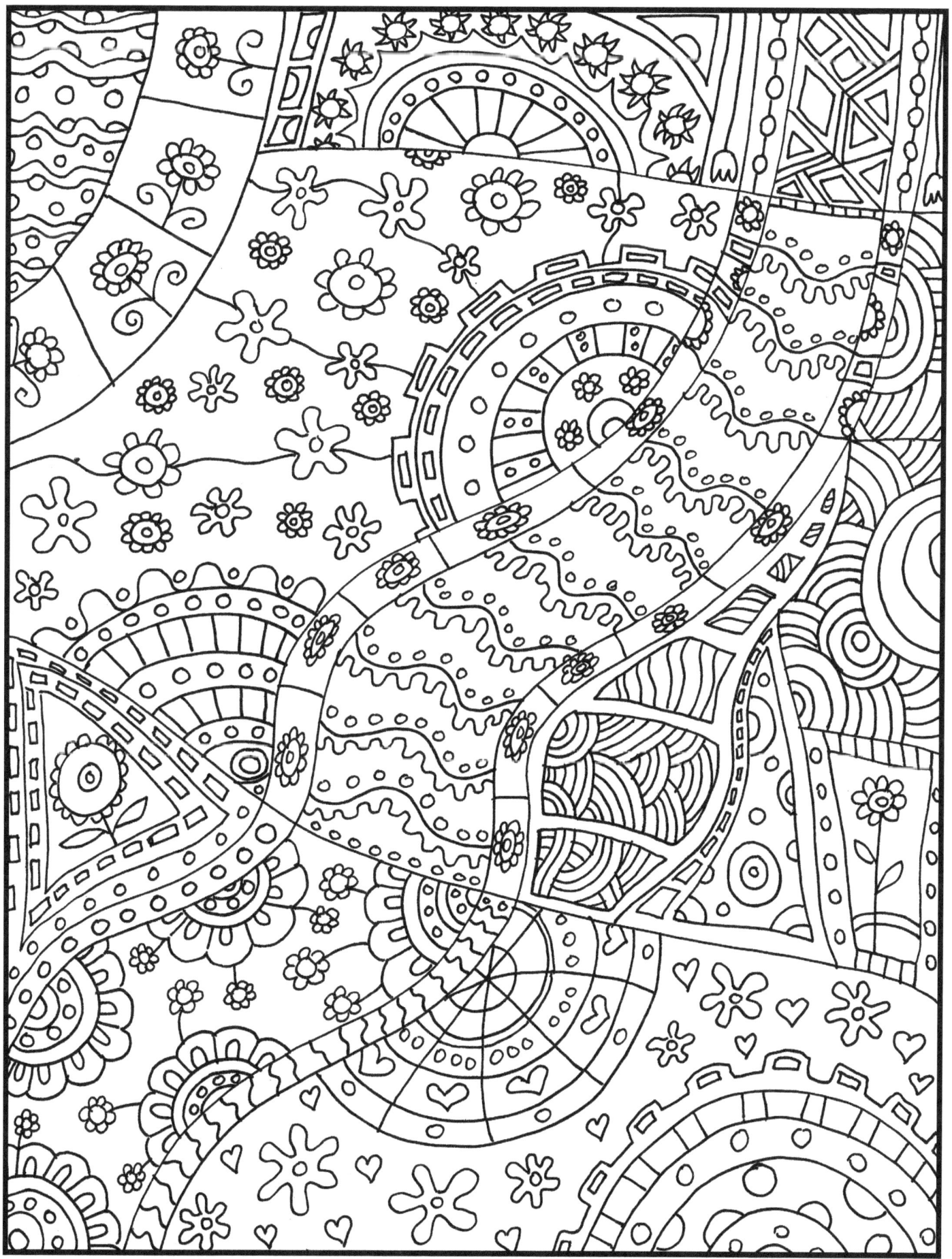

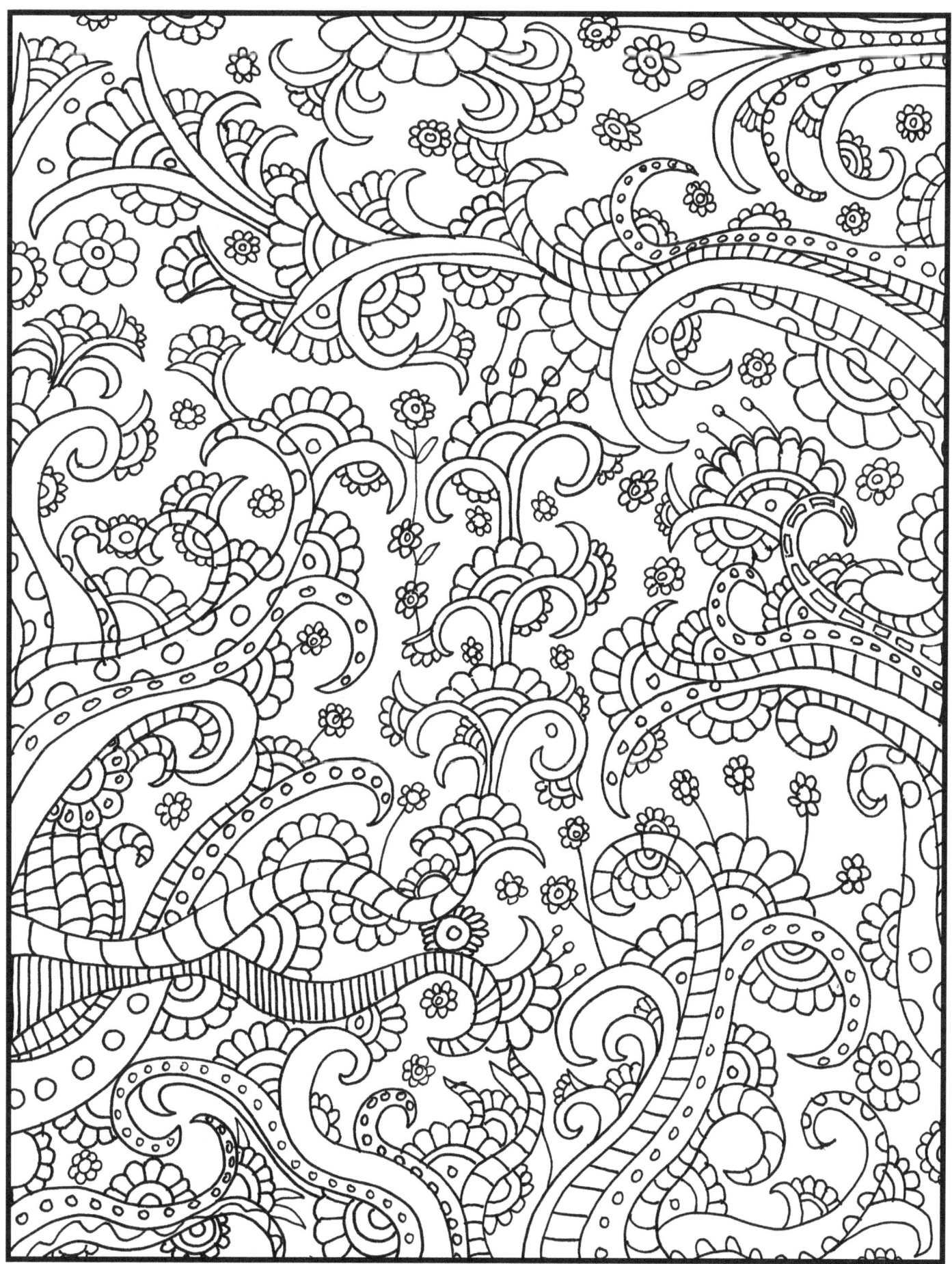

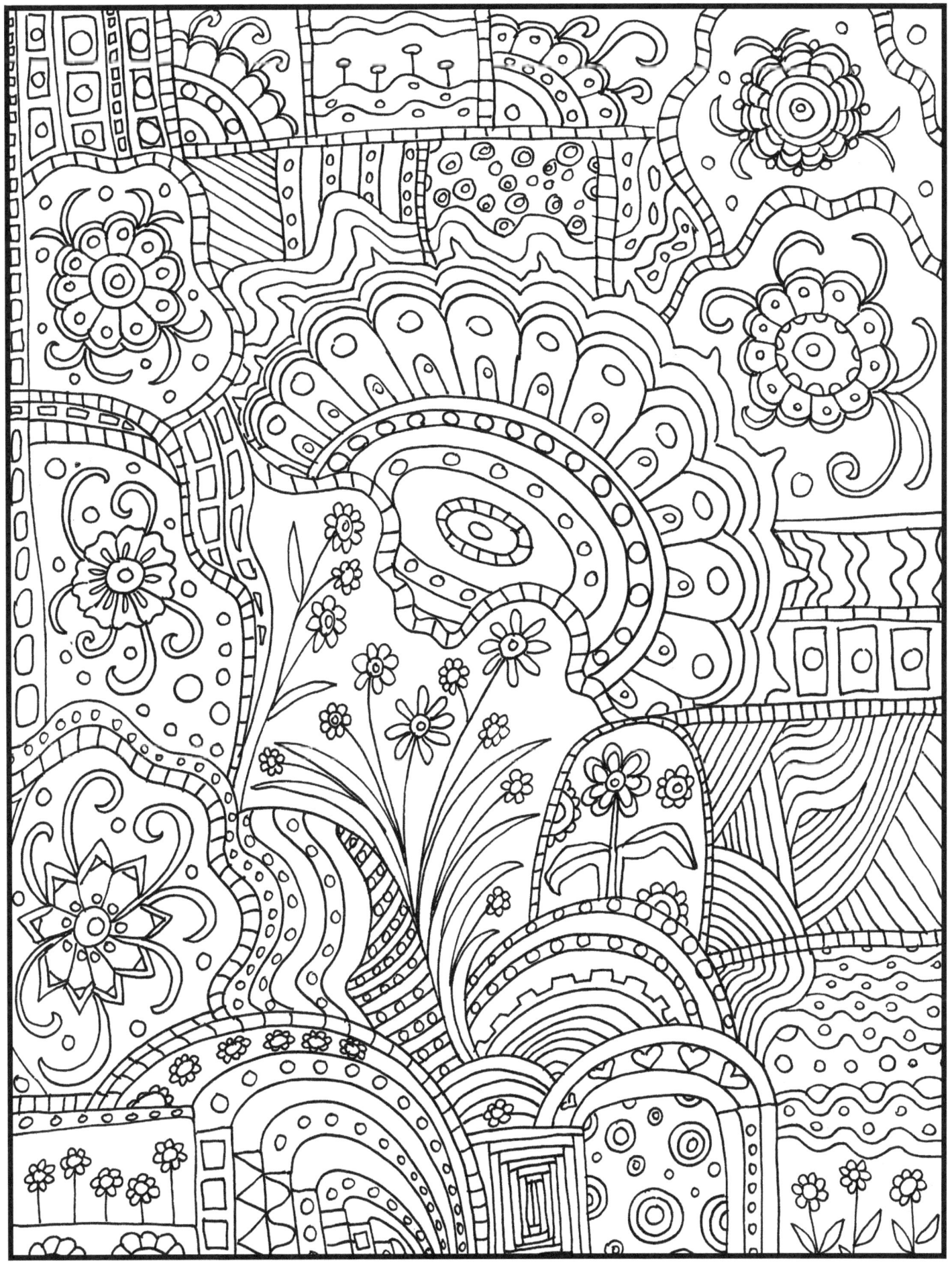

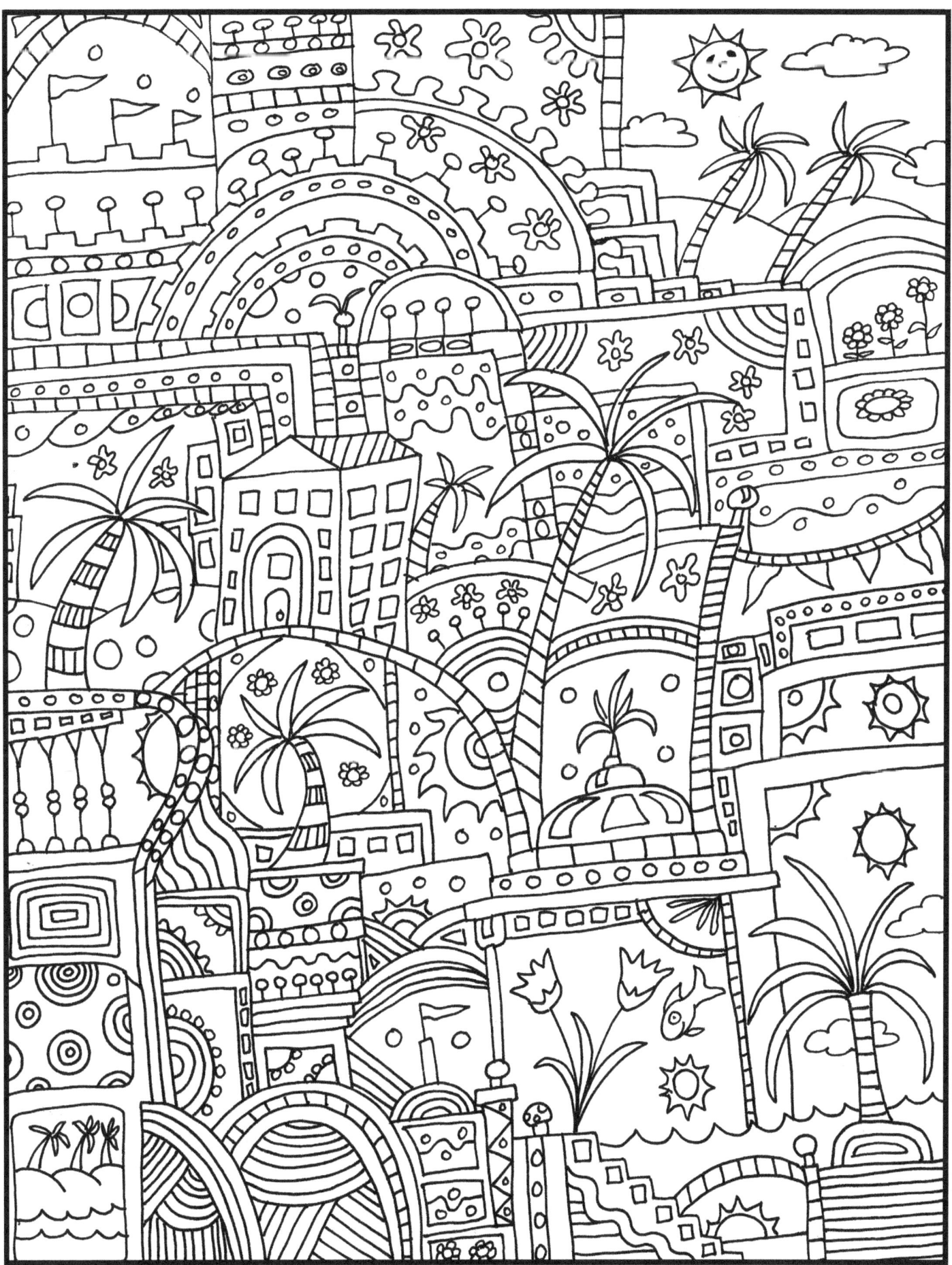

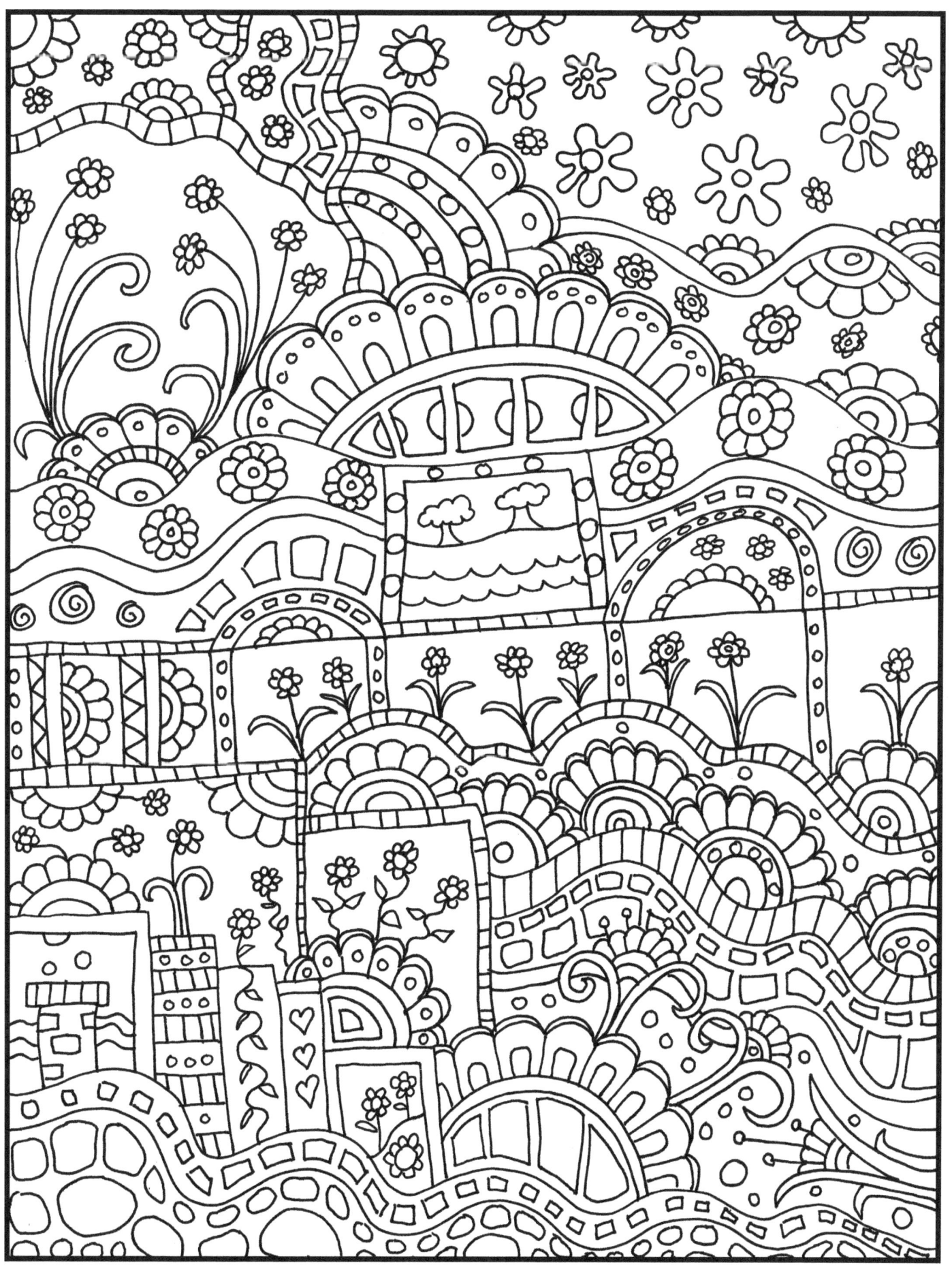

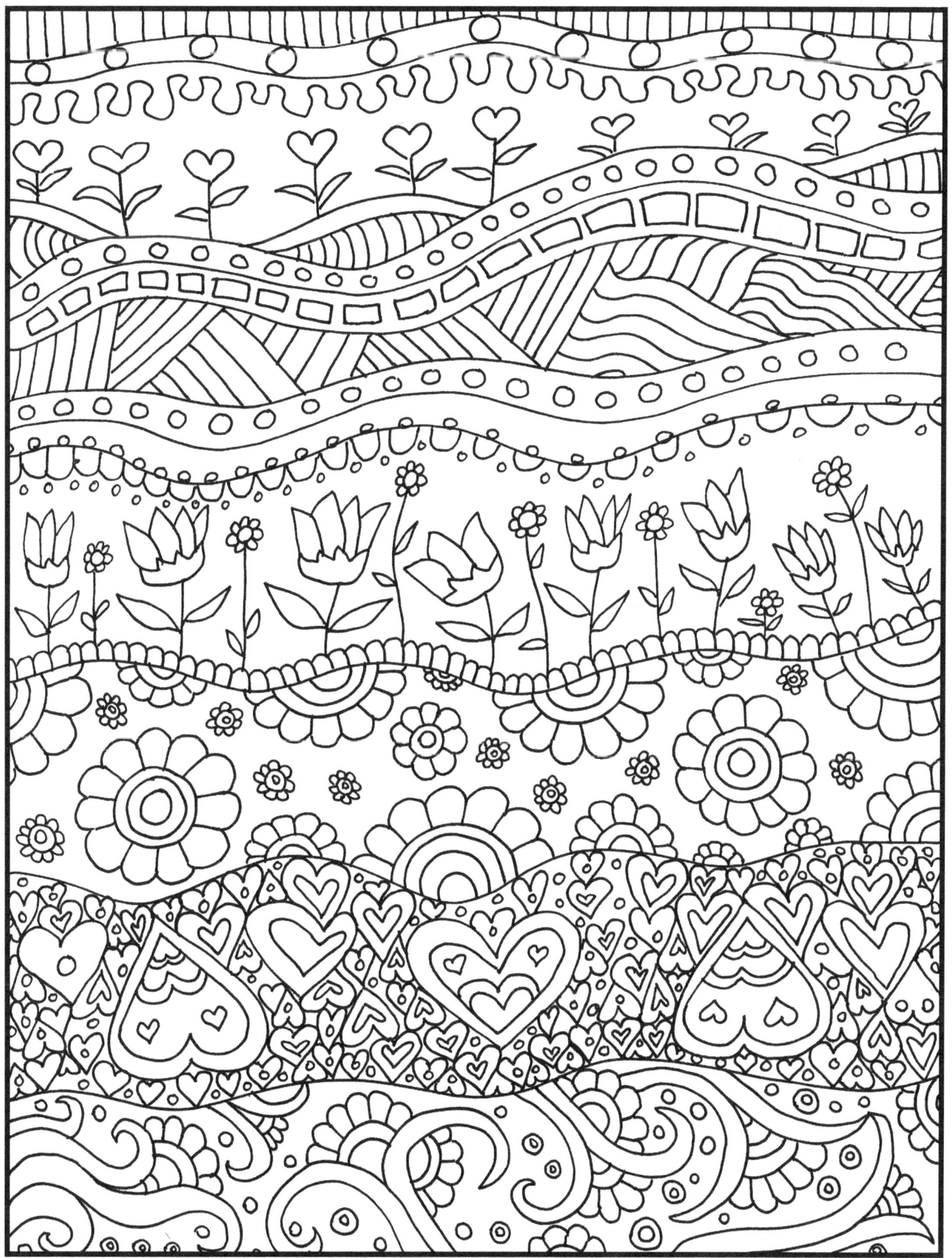

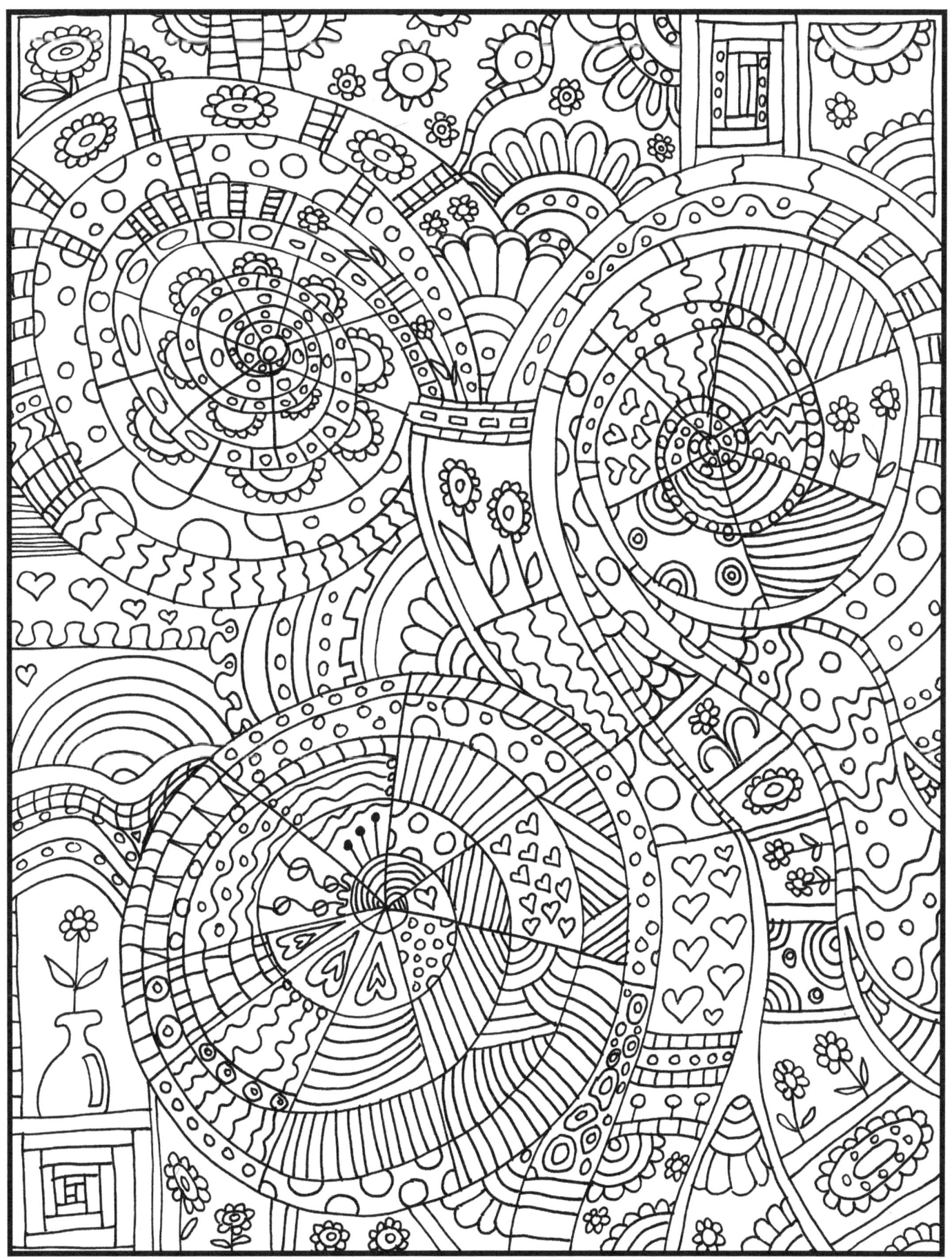

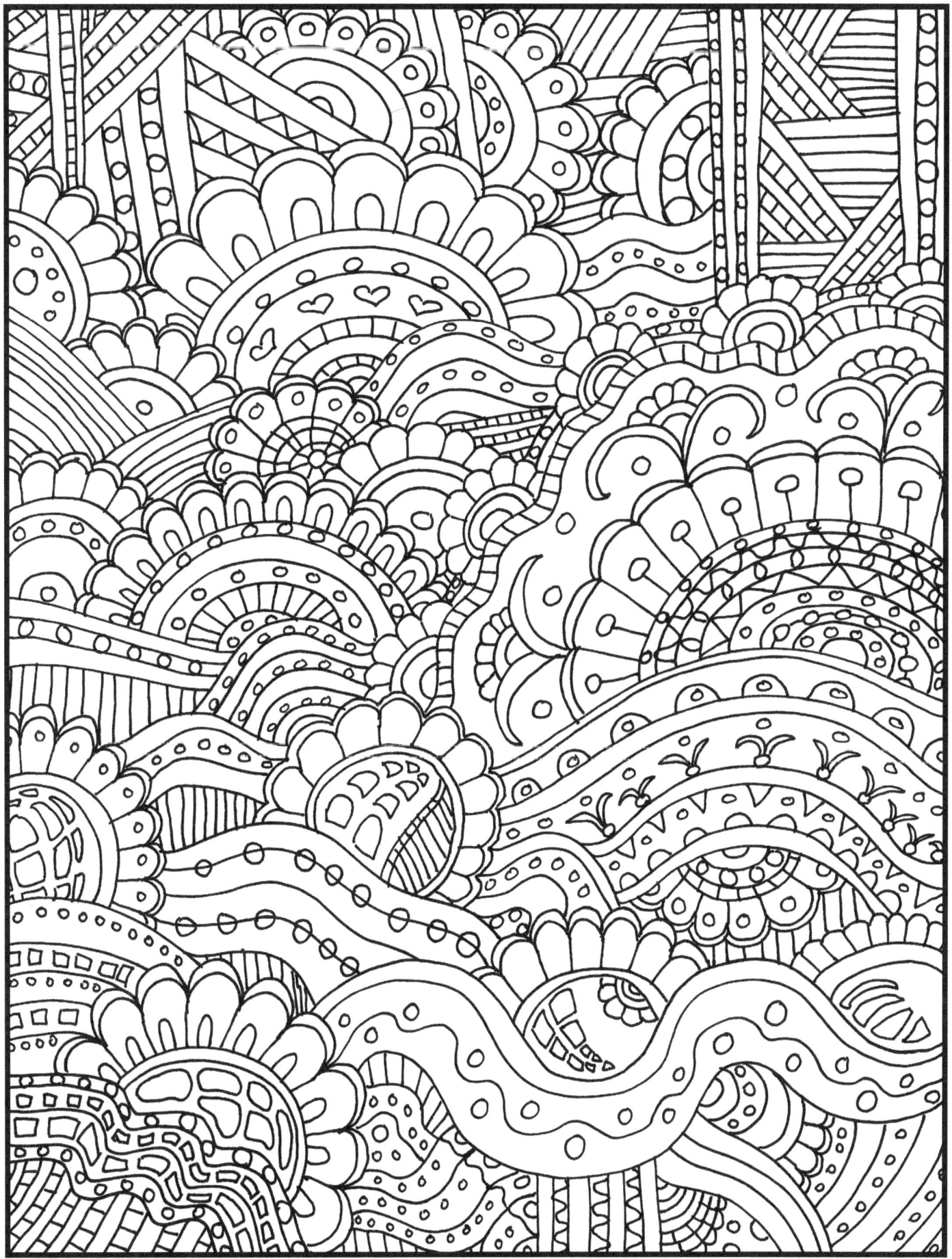

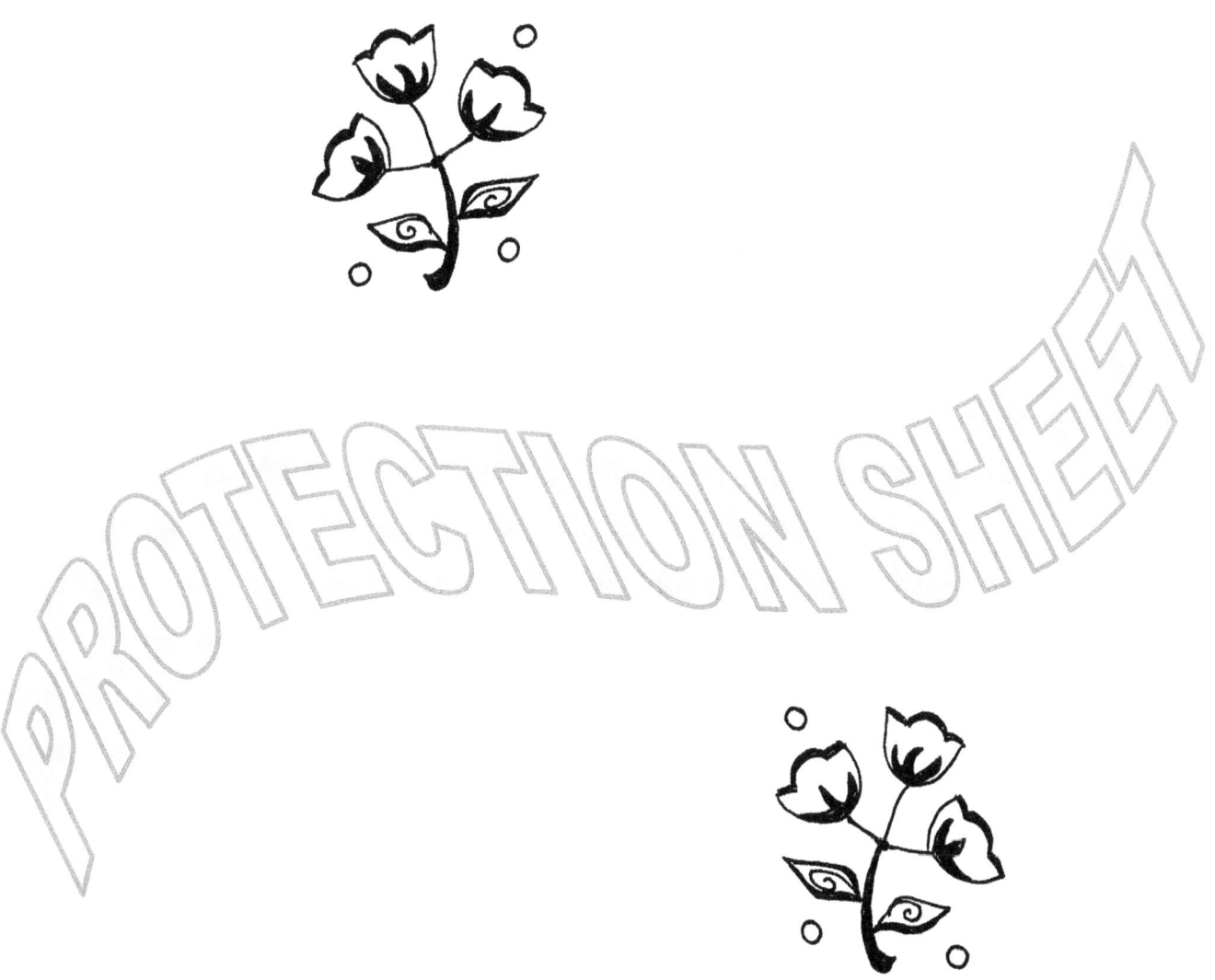

Place this sheet between pages while coloring with markers to prevent bleed-through.

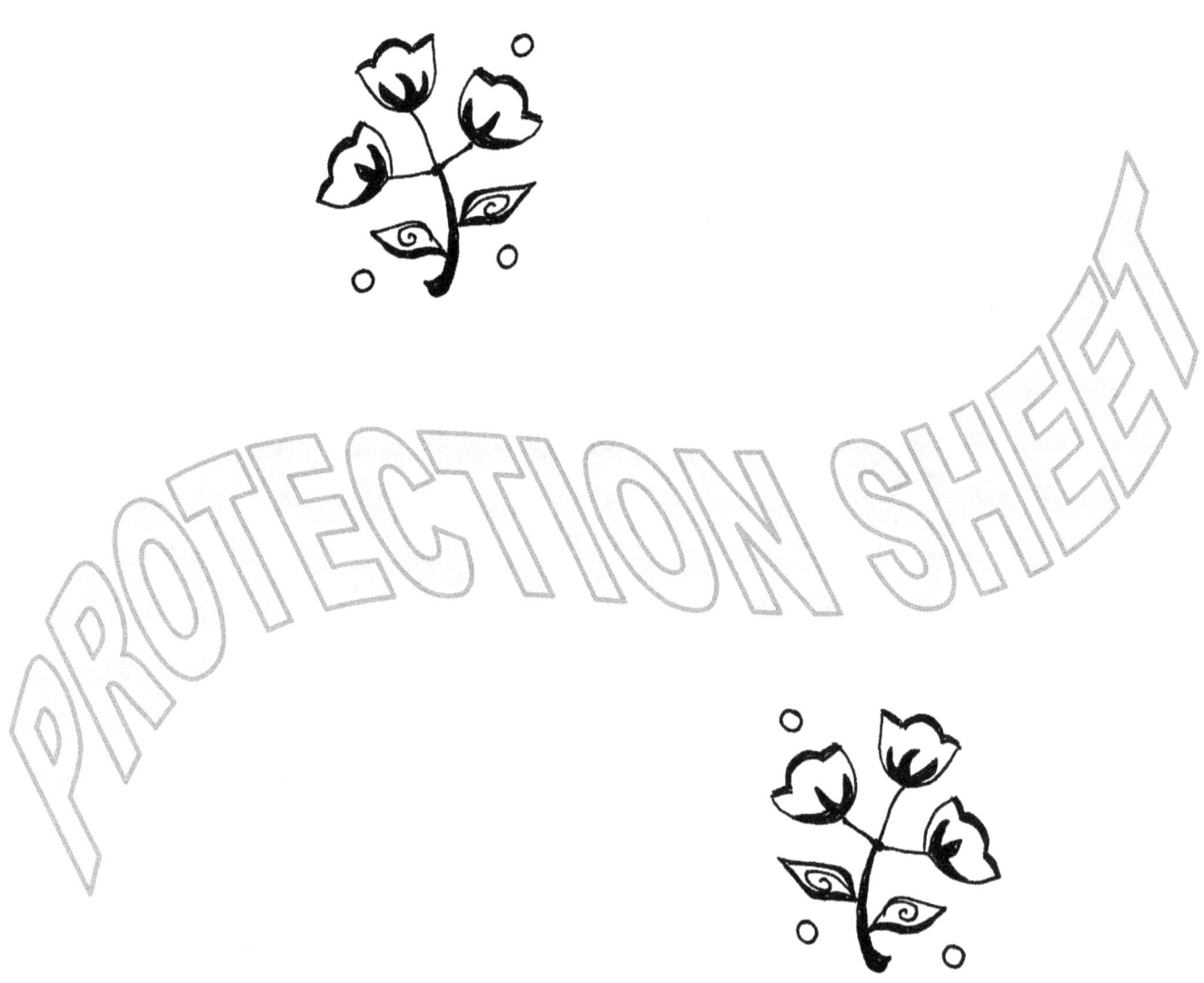

Place this sheet between pages while coloring with markers to prevent bleed-through.

www.ingramcontent.com/pod-product-compliance
Lightning Source LLC
Chambersburg PA
CBHW080836180526
45168CB00006B/2708